IRISH
CHURCH PRAISE

———

An Authorized Supplement
to the 1960 Edition of the
Irish Church Hymnal

———

MUSIC EDITION

ASSOCIATION FOR
PROMOTING CHRISTIAN KNOWLEDGE

OXFORD UNIVERSITY PRESS

1990

Jointly published by
Association for Promoting Christian Knowledge, Dublin
and
Oxford University Press, Walton Street, Oxford OX2 6DP
Oxford New York
Athens Auckland Bangkok Bombay
Calcutta Cape Town Dar es Salaam Delhi
Florence Hong Kong Istanbul Karachi
Kuala Lumpur Madras Madrid Melbourne
Mexico City Nairobi Paris Singapore
Taipei Tokyo Toronto
and associated companies in
Berlin Ibadan

Oxford is a trade mark of Oxford University Press

First printed in 1990
Reprinted in 1990 (twice), 1992, 1995

ISBN 0 19 148153 X

Printed in Scotland

A Words Edition is also available

This collection of hymns was compiled by a committee set up by resolution of the General Synod of the Church of Ireland in 1987, following a suggestion from the Association for Promoting Christian Knowledge that the *Irish Church Hymnal* should be revised to meet the present needs of the Church. The Committee included nominees of the Standing Committee of the General Synod and of the APCK. The 1988 General Synod accepted the recommendation of the Committee that a broadly-based supplement to the *Irish Church Hymnal* should be compiled, submitted to the House of Bishops for approval, and published as soon as practicable, without prejudice to the later revision of the Hymnal.

CONTENTS

FOREWORD

by the Archbishop of Armagh and Primate of All Ireland,
The Most Reverend R. H. A. Eames

I have pleasure in commending this collection of hymns for use throughout the Church of Ireland. It is obvious that a great deal of thought and research has gone into its preparation, and I hope the book will be used regularly and widely in all our churches.

The Church of Ireland has a long and illustrious musical tradition. Many of our hymn-writers have found international acceptance and approval. The depth of spirituality, which has long been an integral part of our ethos, has been evident in the hymns used in parish churches throughout Ireland. But passing years have produced different attitudes to the ways in which we express our love for God in worship. This book takes account of such developments, and in it you will find hymns from a wide range of different sources. It is helpful to have some of the most popular of modern hymns included in one book. I am sure their use will add to the contemporary expression of the Faith we hold.

The House of Bishops welcomes the publication of this book and believes that clergy and parishioners alike will find in it much to enrich and renew their worship.

✠ ROBERT ARMAGH

PREFACE

The compilers of any collection of hymns and songs for use in public worship cannot fail to be aware of the enormous range of musical and literary tastes and styles of worship to be found in our churches. The 'explosion' in hymnody during recent years might have made the preparation of this book a difficult task, but there are many modern hymns which deservedly have already found their way into the worshipping life of the Church and which are worthy of wide use in the Church of Ireland. There are also older hymns which were excluded from former editions of the *Irish Church Hymnal* for some reason or another, and which can still be used with great spiritual profit.

Our aim from the outset, therefore, has been to create a happy blend of the old and new in one book, and to include not only hymns from other countries, traditions, and cultures, but also hymns and tunes with a specifically Irish flavour and character. At the 1989 General Synod there was an overwhelming request that there should be a few hymns written in the Irish language included with our selection. Accordingly, four such hymns have been included, together with English singing translations so that they can be sung by all members of the Church of Ireland.

We are conscious of the growing expectation that worship should be expressed in inclusive language, and we have therefore endeavoured to remove any sexist terminology. Some authors, themselves aware of the increasing need for this, have already adjusted their hymns accordingly. Sometimes, however, poetic style and meaning can be damaged when the wording is changed, and in the few hymns where this might have been the case we have decided that no alterations should be made.

The book has been compiled with both congregations and choirs in mind and to suit all varieties of worship, ranging from the formal to the informal. Many of the tunes are already well known or, at least, traditional in style. These, naturally enough, are best accompanied on the organ. Others, in a folk or popular idiom, have been presented (where possible) in such a way as to be playable on the organ, though it should be recognized that they benefit from the use of guitar(s), piano, percussion, and, indeed, any other available instruments. Therefore, while many of the hymns have been provided with vocal harmonies, guitar chords have also been supplied where appropriate, in the hope that the book will have the widest possible use. We have adopted the policy that hymns are normally intended for singing either in harmony or unison, except where otherwise indicated by the word 'unison'. Since resources in some churches are limited, we have been generous with our suggestions of well-known tunes as alternatives to those given here.

This book is in no way intended to supersede the existing *Irish Church Hymnal*, but rather to supplement those hymns which are regularly used in our churches, and to cater for modern trends in public worship. It was originally in our mind to number the hymns consecutively from the current edition of the *Irish Church Hymnal*, but we decided against this, as we were anxious that this book would be seen not only as a supplement, but as a hymnal which stands in its own right and which could profitably be used elsewhere.

The producers of this supplement are grateful to all who offered help, advice, and support during its preparation. It is our hope that *Irish Church Praise* will be an effective vehicle in lifting our hearts to God, and we are grateful for the privilege of being associated with its production.

✝ EDWARD F. DARLING   *General Editor*

W. DONALD DAVISON, ANTHONY F. CARVER   *Music Editors*

1

HYMNS RELATING TO
THE LECTIONARY
AND FOR
GENERAL USE

1 *Alleluia, alleluia*

ALLELUIA No. 1

Donald Fishel (b. 1928)
arr. Anthony F. Carver
and Donald Davison

Rich and broad

DESCANT *(after vv. 3, 4, 5 – optional)*

Al - le - lu - ia, al - le - lu - ia, give_ thanks to the ris - en Lord! Al - le -

REFRAIN *(Unison)*

- lu - ia, al - le - lu - ia, give_ praise to his name.

VERSES *(Optional harmony)*

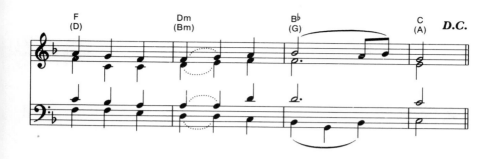

Alleluia, alleluia, give thanks to the risen Lord!
Alleluia, alleluia, give praise to his name.

1 Jesus is Lord of all the earth.
  He is the King of creation.

2 Spread the good news through all the earth,
  Jesus has died and has risen:

3 We have been crucified with Christ—
  now we shall live for ever:

4 God has proclaimed the just reward—
  life for the world, alleluia!

5 Come, let us praise the living God,
  joyfully sing to our Saviour!

Donald Fishel (b. 1928)

2 *Amazing grace*

AMAZING GRACE   CM

Popular variant of early American melody
arr. Donald Davison

Broad and dignified

4

1 Amazing grace (how sweet the sound!)
that saved a wretch like me!
I once was lost, but now am found;
was blind, but now I see.

2 'Twas grace that taught my heart to fear,
and grace my fears relieved;
how precious did that grace appear
the hour I first believed!

3 Through many dangers, toils and snares
I have already come;
'tis grace has brought me safe thus far,
and grace will lead me home.

4 The Lord has promised good to me,
his word my hope secures;
he will my shield and portion be
as long as life endures.

5 Yes, when this flesh and heart shall fail,
and mortal life shall cease,
I shall possess within the veil
a life of joy and peace.

John Newton (1725–1807)

3 *And can it be*

SAGINA 88 88 88   Thomas Campbell (1825–76)

(Repeat lines 5 & 6)

1 And can it be that I should gain
  an interest in the Saviour's blood?
  Died he for me, who caused his pain?
  For me, who him to death pursued?
  Amazing love! how can it be
  that thou, my God, shouldst die for me! } *twice (etc.)*

2 He left his Father's throne above—
  so free, so infinite his grace—
  emptied himself of all but love,
  and bled for Adam's helpless race.
  'Tis mercy all, immense and free;
  for, O my God, it found out me!

3 Long my imprisoned spirit lay
  fast bound in sin and nature's night;
  thine eye diffused a quickening ray—
  I woke, the dungeon flamed with light;
  my chains fell off, my heart was free.
  I rose, went forth, and followed thee.

4 No condemnation now I dread;
  Jesus, and all in him, is mine!
  Alive in him, my living head,
  and clothed in righteousness divine,
  bold I approach the eternal throne,
  and claim the crown, through Christ, my own.

Charles Wesley (1707–88)

7

4 *A new commandment*

A New Commandment

Anon.
arr. Anthony F. Carver

John 13: 34–5

5 *As the deer*

AS THE DEER

Martin Nystrom

Flowing

You a - lone are my strength, my shield, to

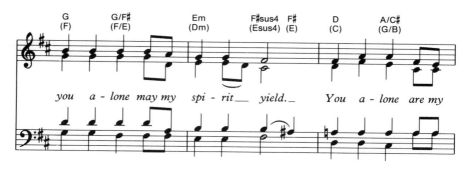

you a - lone may my spi - rit___ yield.__ You a - lone are my

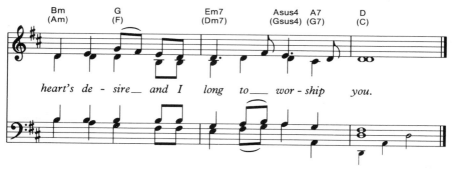

heart's de - sire___ and I long to___ wor - ship you.

1 As the deer pants for the water,
   so my soul longs after you.
   You alone are my heart's desire
   and I long to worship you.

   You alone are my strength, my shield,
   to you alone may my spirit yield.
   You alone are my heart's desire
   and I long to worship you.

2 I want you more than gold or silver,
   only you can satisfy.
   You alone are the real joy-giver
   and the apple of my eye.

3 You're my friend and you are my brother,
   even though you are a king.
   I love you more than any other,
   so much more than anything.

Martin Nystrom

6 *Awake, awake*

Morning Song   86 86 86

American traditional melody
from *The Union Harmony* (Virginia, 1848)
arr. Anthony F. Carver and Donald Davison

1 Awake, awake to love and work!
The lark is in the sky,
the fields are wet with diamond dew,
the world's awake to cry
their blessings on the Lord of life,
as he goes meekly by.

2 Come, let thy voice be one with theirs,
shout with their shout of praise;
see how the giant sun soars up,
great lord of years and days;
so let the love of Jesus come,
and set thy soul ablaze.

3 To give, and give, and give again,
what God has given thee;
to spend thyself, nor count the cost;
to serve right gloriously
the God who gave all worlds that are
and all that are to be.

Geoffrey Anketell Studdert-Kennedy
(1883–1929)

7 Be still

BE STILL

Dave Evans

Reverently
Unison

1. Be still, for the pre-sence of the Lord, the
Ho - ly One is here. Come, bow be -
- fore him now, with rev - er - ence and
fear. In him no sin is found,

1 Be still, for the presence of the Lord, the Holy One is here.
Come, bow before him now, with reverence and fear.
In him no sin is found, we stand on holy ground.
Be still, for the presence of the Lord, the Holy One is here.

2 Be still, for the glory of the Lord is shining all around;
he burns with holy fire, with splendour he is crowned.
How awesome is the sight, our radiant King of light!
Be still, for the glory of the Lord is shining all around.

3 Be still, for the power of the Lord is moving in this place,
he comes to cleanse and heal, to minister his grace.
No work too hard for him, in faith receive from him;
be still, for the power of the Lord is moving in this place.

Dave Evans
based on Exodus 3: 1–6

8 Be still, my soul

FINLANDIA   10 10 10 10 10 10

From the symphonic poem *Finlandia* by
Jean Sibelius (1865–1957)

This tune may also be used for 'Long did I toil, and knew no earthly rest' (*Irish Church Hymnal* No. 646).

Stille, mein Wille; dein Jesus hilft siegen

1 Be still, my soul: the Lord is on thy side;
  bear patiently the cross of grief or pain;
  leave to thy God to order and provide;
  in every change he faithful will remain.
  Be still, my soul: thy best, thy heavenly friend
  through thorny ways leads to a joyful end.

2 Be still, my soul: thy God doth undertake
  to guide the future as he has the past.
  Thy hope, thy confidence let nothing shake;
  all now mysterious shall be bright at last.
  Be still, my soul: the waves and winds still know
  his voice who ruled them while he dwelt below.

3 Be still, my soul: when dearest friends depart,
  and all is darkened in the vale of tears,
  then shalt thou better know his love, his heart,
  who comes to soothe thy sorrow and thy fears.
  Be still, my soul: thy Jesus can repay,
  from his own fullness, all he takes away.

4 Be still, my soul: the hour is hastening on
  when we shall be forever with the Lord,
  when disappointment, grief, and fear are gone,
  sorrow forgot, love's purest joys restored.
  Be still, my soul: when change and tears are past,
  all safe and blessèd we shall meet at last.

Katharina von Schlegel (1697–?)
tr. Jane Laurie Borthwick (1813–97)

9 *Be strong in the Lord*

LAUDATE DOMINUM   55 55 65 65

Charles Hubert Hastings Parry
(1848–1918)

May also be sung to HANOVER (*Irish Church Hymnal* No. 352).

1 Be strong in the Lord
in armour of light!
With helmet and sword,
with shield for the fight;
on prayer be dependent,
be belted and shod,
in breastplate resplendent—
the armour of God.

2 Integrity gird
you round to impart
the truth of his word
as truth in your heart:
his righteousness wearing
as breastplate of mail,
his victory sharing,
be strong to prevail.

3 With eagerness shod
stand firm in your place,
or go forth for God
with news of his grace:
no foe shall disarm you
nor force you to yield,
no arrow can harm you
with faith as your shield.

4 Though Satan presume
to test you and try,
in helmet and plume
your head shall be high:
beset by temptation
be true to your Lord,
your helmet salvation
and scripture your sword.

5 So wield well your blade,
rejoice in its powers!
Fight on undismayed
for Jesus is ours!
Then in him victorious
your armour lay down,
to praise, ever glorious,
his cross and his crown.

Timothy Dudley-Smith (b. 1926)
based on Ephesians 6: 10–18

10 *Bind us together*

BIND US TOGETHER   Bob Gillman

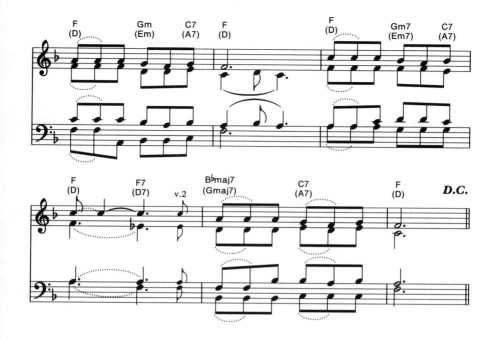

Bind us together, Lord,
bind us together
with cords that cannot be broken.
Bind us together, Lord,
bind us together,
O bind us together with love.

1 There is only one God.
 There is only one King.
 There is only one body;
 that is why we sing.

2 Made for the glory of God,
 purchased by his precious Son.
 Born with the right to be clean,
 for Jesus the victory has won.

3 You are the family of God.
 You are the promise divine.
 You are God's chosen desire.
 You are the glorious new wine.

Bob Gillman

21

11 *Christ be beside me*

BUNESSAN 55 54 D

Scots Gaelic traditional melody
arr. Donald Davison

For another version (with guitar chords) see No. 59. See also *Irish Church Hymnal* No. 56.

1 Christ be beside me,
Christ be before me,
Christ be behind me,
King of my heart.
Christ be within me,
Christ be below me,
Christ be above me,
never to part.

2 Christ on my right hand,
Christ on my left hand,
Christ all around me,
shield in the strife.
Christ in my sleeping,
Christ in my sitting,
Christ in my rising,
light of my life.

3 Christ be in all hearts
thinking about me,
Christ be on all tongues
telling of me.
Christ be the vision
in eyes that see me,
in ears that hear me,
Christ ever be.

James Quinn (b. 1919)
adapted from 'St Patrick's Breastplate'

12 Christel is alive!

TRURO LM

Melody from Thomas Williams's
Psalmodia Evangelica (1789)

For another harmonization of this tune (in D major) see *Irish Church Hymnal* No. 421.

1 Christ is alive! Let Christians sing;
the cross stands empty to the sky;
let streets and homes with praises ring;
love drowned in death shall never die.

2 Christ is alive! No longer bound
to distant years in Palestine;
but saving, healing, here and now,
and touching every place and time.

3 Not throned afar, remotely high,
untouched, unmoved by human pains,
but daily, in the midst of life,
our Saviour in the Godhead reigns.

4 In every insult, rift and war,
where colour, scorn or wealth divide,
he suffers still, yet loves the more,
and lives where even hope has died.

5 Christ is alive, and comes to bring
new life to this and every age,
till earth and all creation ring
with joy, with justice, love, and praise.

Brian Arthur Wren (b. 1936)

23

13 *Christ triumphant*

GUITING POWER   85 85 78   John Barnard (b. 1948)

5. Our hearts and voi - ces rais - ing through the a - ges long, up - on you gaz - ing, this shall be — our song: *Yours the glo - ry and the*

May also be sung to ANGEL VOICES (*Irish Church Hymnal* No. 474) or ARTHOG (No. 14).

1 Christ triumphant, ever reigning,
  Saviour, Master, King!
  Lord of heaven, our lives sustaining,
  hear us as we sing:

  Yours the glory and the crown,
  the high renown, th'eternal name!

2 Word incarnate, truth revealing,
  Son of Man on earth!
  Power and majesty concealing
  by your humble birth:

3 Suffering servant, scorned, ill-treated,
  victim crucified!
  Death is through the cross defeated,
  sinners justified:

4 Priestly king, enthroned for ever
  high in heaven above!
  Sin and death and hell shall never
  stifle hymns of love:

5 So, our hearts and voices raising
  through the ages long,
  ceaselessly upon you gazing,
  this shall be our song:

Michael John Saward (b. 1932)

14 *Come to us, creative Spirit*

ARTHOG 85 85 87   George Thalben-Ball (1896–1987)

May also be sung to ANGEL VOICES (*Irish Church Hymnal* No. 474).

26

1 Come to us, creative Spirit,
in our Father's house;
every human talent hallow,
hidden skills arouse,
that within your earthly temple,
wise and simple
may rejoice.

2 Poet, painter, music-maker
all your treasures bring;
craftsman, actor, graceful dancer
make your offering;
join your hands in celebration:
let creation
shout and sing!

3 Word from God eternal springing
fill our minds, we pray;
and in all artistic vision
give integrity:
may the flame within us burning
kindle yearning
day by day.

4 In all places and forever
glory be expressed
to the Son, with God the Father
and the Spirit blessed:
in our worship and our living
keep us striving
for the best.

David Mowbray (b. 1938)

15 *Fairest Lord Jesus*

SCHÖNSTER HERR JESU   569 558   Silesian folk-song (1842)

Schönster Herr Jesu

1 Fairest Lord Jesus,
  Lord of all creation,
  Jesus, of God and Mary the Son;
  you will I cherish,
  you will I honour,
  you are my soul's delight and crown.

2 Fair are the meadows,
  fairer still the woodlands,
  robed in the verdure and bloom of spring.
  Jesus is fairer,
  Jesus is purer,
  he makes the saddest heart to sing.

3 Fair are the flowers,
  fairer still the children,
  in all the freshness of youth arrayed:
  yet is their beauty
  fading and fleeting;
  my Jesus, yours will never fade.

4 Fair is the sunshine,
  fairer still the moonlight
  and fair the twinkling starry host.
  Jesus shines brighter,
  Jesus shines clearer
  than all the stars that heaven can boast.

5 All fairest beauty.
  heavenly and earthly,
  wondrously, Jesus, in you I see;
  none can be nearer,
  fairer or dearer,
  than you, my Saviour, are to me.

from the German (Münster, 1677)
tr. Lilian Sinclair Stevenson (1870–1960)
and others

16 *Father, Lord of all creation*

ABBOT'S LEIGH   87 87 D

Cyril Vincent Taylor (b. 1907)

May also be sung to RUSTINGTON (No. 133).

1 Father, Lord of all creation,
  ground of being, life and love;
  height and depth beyond description
  only life in you can prove:
  you are mortal life's dependence:
  thought, speech, sight are ours by grace;
  yours is every hour's existence,
  sovereign Lord of time and space.

2 Jesus Christ, the Man for others,
  we, your people, make our prayer:
  help us love—as sisters, brothers—
  all whose burdens we can share.
  Where your name binds us together
  you, Lord Christ, will surely be;
  where no selfishness can sever
  there your love the world may see.

3 Holy Spirit, rushing, burning
  wind and flame of Pentecost,
  fire our hearts afresh with yearning
  to regain what we have lost.
  May your love unite our action,
  nevermore to speak alone:
  God, in us abolish faction,
  God, through us your love make known.

Stewart Cross (1928–89)

17 *Father, now behold us*

GLENFINLAS 65 65   Kenneth George Finlay (1882–1974)

May also be sung to ST BARNABAS (*Irish Church Hymnal* No. 453).

For the Baptism of a child

1 Father, now behold us
  and this child, we pray:
  in your love enfold us,
  wash our sins away.

2 Christ's eternal blessing
  for this life we claim:
  faith, by ours, professing;
  signed in Jesus' Name.

3 By the Spirit tended
  childhood grow to youth,
  from all ill defended,
  full of grace and truth.

4 God of all creation,
  stoop from heaven's throne,
  and by Christ's salvation
  make this child your own.

Timothy Dudley-Smith (b. 1926)

18 *Father, we adore you*

FATHER, WE ADORE YOU

Terrye Coelho

May be sung as a round, the parts entering where indicated.

1 Father, we adore you,
   lay our lives before you:
   how we love you!

2 Jesus, we adore you,
   lay our lives before you:
   how we love you!

3 Spirit, we adore you,
   lay our lives before you:
   how we love you!

Terrye Coelho

19 *Father of mercy*

GERARD 11 11 11 5

Arthur Hutchings (1906–89)

May also be sung to CHRISTE SANCTORUM, NEWMINSTER ABBEY, or ISTE CONFESSOR
(*Irish Church Hymnal* Nos. 21 and 423*i* and *ii*).

1 Father of mercy, God of consolation,
  look on your people, gathered here to praise you,
  pity our weakness, come in power to aid us,
  source of all blessing.

2 Son of the Father, Lord of all creation,
  come as our Saviour, Jesus, friend of sinners,
  grant us forgiveness, lift our downcast spirit,
  heal us and save us.

3 Life-giving Spirit, be our light in darkness,
  come to befriend us, help us bear our burdens,
  give us true courage, breathe your peace around us,
  stay with us always.

4 God in Three Persons, Father, Son and Spirit,
  come to renew us, fill your Church with glory,
  grant us your healing, pledge of resurrection,
  foretaste of heaven.

James Quinn (b. 1919)

While of general use also, this hymn is specially suitable
at the laying-on-of-hands or anointing of the sick.

20 Finished the strife of battle

SURREXIT 88 88

A. Gregory Murray (b. 1905)

Al-le-lu-ia, al-le-lu - ia!

1 Finished the strife of battle now,
   gloriously crowned the victor's brow:
   sing with gladness, hence with sadness:

   Alleluia, alleluia!

2 After the death that him befell,
   Jesus Christ has harrowed hell:
   songs of praising we are raising:

3 On the third morning he arose,
   shining with victory o'er his foes;
   earth is singing, heaven is ringing:

4 Lord, by your wounds on you we call:
   now that from death you've freed us all:
   may our living be thanksgiving:

Latin hymn, ? 17th cent.
tr. John Mason Neale (1818–66)

21 Forth in the peace of Christ we go

DUKE STREET LM

Late 18th-century melody
attrib. J. L. Hatton (d. 1793)

For another harmonization of this tune see *Irish Church Hymnal* No. 530.

1 Forth in the peace of Christ we go;
Christ to the world with joy we bring;
Christ in our minds, Christ on our lips,
Christ in our hearts, the world's true King.

2 King of our hearts, Christ makes us kings;
kingship with him his servants gain;
with Christ, the Servant-Lord of all,
Christ's world we serve to share Christ's reign.

3 Priests of the world, Christ sends us forth
this world of time to consecrate,
our world of sin by grace to heal,
Christ's world in Christ to re-create.

4 Prophets of Christ, we hear his word:
he claims our minds, to search his ways,
he claims our lips, to speak his truth,
he claims our hearts, to sing his praise.

5 We are his Church, he makes us one:
here is one hearth for all to find,
here is one flock, one Shepherd-King,
here is one faith, one heart, one mind.

James Quinn (b. 1919)

22 *For the fruits of his creation*

EAST ACKLAM   84 84 888 4   Francis Jackson (b. 1917)

May also be sung to AR HYD Y NOS (*Irish Church Hymnal* No. 16).

1 For the fruits of his creation,
thanks be to God!
For his gifts to every nation,
thanks be to God!
For the ploughing, sowing, reaping,
silent growth while we are sleeping;
future needs in earth's safe keeping,
thanks be to God!

2 In the just reward of labour,
God's will is done;
in the help we give our neighbour,
God's will is done;
in our worldwide task of caring
for the hungry and despairing;
in the harvests we are sharing,
God's will is done.

3 For the harvests of the Spirit,
thanks be to God!
For the good we all inherit,
thanks be to God!
For the wonders that astound us,
for the truths that still confound us;
most of all, that love has found us,
thanks be to God!

Frederick Pratt Green (b. 1903)

23 *From heaven you came*
(The Servant King)

THE SERVANT KING

Graham Kendrick (b. 1950)

Worshipfully

1. From heav'n you came, help-less babe, en-ter'd our world, your glo - ry veil'd; not to be served but to serve, and give your life that we might live. *This is our God,___ the Ser-vant King,___ he calls us*

now to fol-low him,_____ to bring our lives as a dai-ly off-er- -ing_____ of wor-ship to_____ the Ser-vant King. King.

1 From heav'n you came, helpless babe,
enter'd our world, your glory veil'd;
not to be served but to serve,
and give your life that we might live.

This is our God, the Servant King,
he calls us now to follow him,
to bring our lives as a daily offering
of worship to the Servant King.

2 There in the garden of tears,
my heavy load he chose to bear;
his heart wth sorrow was torn,
'Yet not my will but yours,' he said.

3 Come see his hands and his feet,
the scars that speak of sacrifice,
hands that flung stars into space
to cruel nails surrendered.

4 So let us learn how to serve,
and in our lives enthrone him;
each other's needs to prefer,
for it is Christ we're serving.

Graham Kendrick (b. 1950)

41

24 *For you are my God*

FOR YOU ARE MY GOD

John B. Foley

Moderate speed

Unison

REFRAIN

For you are my God;___ you a-lone are my joy.___ De-fend me, O Lord.___

VERSES

1. You give mar - vel - lous com - rades to
2. You are my por - tion and
3. Glad are my heart and my
4. You show me the path for my

me:_____ the faith - ful who
cup;_____ it is you that I
soul;_____ se - cure - ly my
life;_____ in your pre - sence the

dwell in your land._____ —
claim for my prize._____ Your
bo - dy shall rest._____ For
ful - ness of joy._____ To

43

John B. Foley, based on Psalm 16

44

25 *Fruitful trees*

BEECHGROVE 87 87   William Donald Davison (b. 1937)

May also be sung to SHIPSTON (No. 120).

1 Fruitful trees, the Spirit's sowing,
   may we ripen and increase,
   fruit to life eternal growing,
   rich in love and joy and peace.

2 Laden branches freely bearing
   gifts the Giver loves to bless;
   here is fruit that grows by sharing,
   patience, kindness, gentleness.

3 Rooted deep in Christ our master,
   Christ our pattern and our goal,
   teach us, as the years fly faster,
   goodness, faith and self-control.

4 Fruitful trees, the Spirit's tending,
   may we grow till harvests cease;
   till we taste, in life unending,
   heaven's love and joy and peace.

Timothy Dudley-Smith (b. 1926)
based on Galatians 5: 22–3

26 *Give me oil in my lamp (joy in my heart)*

SING HOSANNA   10 8 10 9 with refrain

Traditional melody
arr. Donald Davison

The small notes may be substituted for the given bass when pedals are not used.

1 Give me oil in my lamp, keep me burning,
give me oil in my lamp, I pray;
give me oil in my lamp, keep me burning,
keep me burning till the break of day.

Sing hosanna, sing hosanna,
sing hosanna to the King of kings!
Sing hosanna, sing hosanna,
sing hosanna to the King!

2 Give me joy in my heart, keep me praising,
give me joy in my heart, I pray;
give me joy in my heart, keep me praising,
keep me praising till the break of day.

3 Give me peace in my heart, keep me loving,
give me peace in my heart, I pray;
give me peace in my heart, keep me loving,
keep me loving till the break of day.

4 Give me love in my heart, keep me serving,
give me love in my heart, I pray;
give me love in my heart, keep me serving,
keep me serving till the break of day.

Traditional

The first verse may be omitted if desired.

27 Give to us eyes

Don Harper
arr. Anthony F. Carver

*Guitarists may substitute A when playing without keyboard.

1 Give to us eyes
   that we may truly see,
   flight of a bird,
   the shapes in a tree,
   curve of a hillside,
   colours in a stone,
   give to us seeing eyes, O Lord.

2 Give to us ears
   that we may truly hear,
   music in birdsong,
   rippling water clear,
   whine of the winter wind,
   laughter of a friend,
   give to us hearing ears, O Lord.

3 Give to us hands
   that we may truly know,
   patterns in tree bark,
   crispness of the snow,
   smooth feel of velvet,
   shapes in a shell,
   give to us knowing hands, O Lord.

Peggy Blakeley

28 *God forgave my sin*
(Freely, freely)

FREELY, FREELY

Jimmy Owens

He said: Free - ly, free - ly you have re -

(Org. Ped.)

REFRAIN *(Unison or improvised harmony)*

1 God forgave my sin in Jesus' name;
 I've been born again in Jesus' name,
 and in Jesus' name I come to you
 to share his love as he told me to.

   He said:
   Freely, freely you have received,
   freely, freely give;
   go in my name and because you believe,
   others will know that I live.

2 All power is given in Jesus' name,
 in earth and heaven in Jesus' name;
 and in Jesus' name I come to you
 to share his power as he told me to.

Jimmy and Carol Owens

29 *God has spoken*

GOD HAS SPOKEN

Israeli traditional folk-melody
arr. Donald Davison

God   has spo-ken   to   his peo-ple,   hal-le-lu - jah!

And   his words are   words   of wis-dom,   hal-le-lu - jah!

hal-le-lu - jah!

Fine

God has spoken to his people, hallelujah!
And his words are words of wisdom, hallelujah!
God has spoken to his people, hallelujah!
And his words are words of wisdom, hallelujah!

1 Open your ears, O Christian people,
   open your ears and hear good news.
   Open your hearts, O royal priesthood,
   God has come to you. (twice)

2 They who have ears to hear his message,
   they who have ears, then let them hear.
   They who would learn the way of wisdom,
   let them hear God's word. (twice)

3 Israel comes to greet the Saviour,
   Judah is glad to see his day.
   From east and west the peoples travel,
   he will show the way. (twice)

Willard Francis Jabusch (b. 1930)

30 *God is here*

BLAENWERN 87 87 D   William Penfro Rowlands (1860–1937)

For another setting of this tune (in A♭) see *Irish Church Hymnal* No. 590.

1 God is here; as we his people
meet to offer praise and prayer,
may we find in fuller measure
what it is in Christ we share.
Here, as in the world around us,
all our varied skills and arts
wait the coming of his Spirit
into open minds and hearts.

2 Here are symbols to remind us
of our lifelong need of grace;
here are table, font and pulpit,
here the cross has central place;
here in honesty of preaching,
here in silence as in speech,
here in newness and renewal
God the Spirit comes to each.

3 Here our children find a welcome
in the Shepherd's flock and fold,
here, as bread and wine are taken,
Christ sustains us, as of old.
Here the servants of the Servant
seek in worship to explore
what it means in daily living
to believe and to adore.

4 Lord of all, of Church and Kingdom,
in an age of change and doubt
keep us faithful to the gospel,
help us work your purpose out.
Here, in this day's dedication,
all we have to give, receive.
We, who cannot live without you,
we adore you, we believe.

Frederick Pratt Green (b. 1903)

31 *God is love*

PERSONENT HODIE   66 66 6 with refrain

Melody from *Piae Cantiones* (1582)
arr. Donald Davison

For another setting of this tune see No. 50.

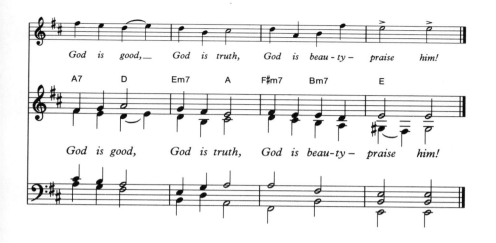

God is good,— God is truth, God is beau-ty – praise him!

A7   D   Em7   A   F#m7   Bm7   E

God is good, God is truth, God is beau-ty – praise him!

1 God is love—his the care,
   tending each, everywhere;
   God is love—all is there!
   Jesus came to show him,
   that we all might know him:

   Sing aloud, loud, loud;
   sing aloud, loud, loud:
   God is good,
   God is truth, God is beauty—praise him!

2 Jesus shared all our pain,
   lived and died, rose again,
   rules our hearts, now as then—
   for he came to save us
   by the truth he gave us:

3 To our Lord praise we sing—
   light and life, friend and king,
   coming down love to bring,
   pattern for our duty,
   showing God in beauty:

Percy Dearmer (1867–1936)
(omitting former verse 2)

57

32 *God of Eve and God of Mary*

FIRST TUNE

DRAKES BROUGHTON 87 87

Edward Elgar (1857–1934)

SECOND TUNE

WYCHBOLD 87 87

Walter G. Whinfield (1865–1919)

May also be sung to SHIPSTON (No. 120).
WYCHBOLD may also be used for 'In the Cross of Christ I glory' (*Irish Church Hymnal* No. 372).

1 God of Eve and God of Mary,
  God of love and mother-earth,
  thank you for the ones who with us
  shared their life and gave us birth.

2 As you came to earth in Jesus,
  so you come to us today;
  you are present in the caring
  that prepares us for life's way.

3 Thank you, that the Church, our mother,
  gives us bread and fills our cup,
  and the comfort of the Spirit
  warms our hearts and lifts us up.

4 Thank you for belonging, shelter,
  bonds of friendship, ties of blood,
  and for those who have no children,
  yet are parents under God.

5 God of Eve and God of Mary,
  Christ our brother, human Son,
  Spirit, caring like a mother,
  take our love and make us one!

Frederik Herman Kaan (b. 1929)

33 *Go forth and tell!*

YANWORTH 10 10 10 10   John Barnard (b. 1948)

May also be sung to WOODLANDS (Nos. 125 or 136).

60

1 Go forth and tell! O Church of God, awake!
   God's saving news to all the nations take:
   proclaim Christ Jesus, Saviour, Lord, and King,
   that all the world his worthy praise may sing.

2 Go forth and tell! God's love embraces all;
   he will in grace respond to all who call:
   how shall they call if they have never heard
   the gracious invitation of his word?

3 Go forth and tell! Where still the darkness lies
   in wealth or want, the sinner surely dies:
   give us, O Lord, concern of heart and mind,
   a love like yours which cares for humankind.

4 Go forth and tell! The doors are open wide:
   share God's good gifts—let no one be denied;
   live out your life as Christ your Lord shall choose,
   your ransomed powers for his sole glory use.

5 Go forth and tell! O Church of God, arise!
   Go in the strength which Christ your Lord supplies;
   go till all nations his great name adore
   and serve him, Lord and King for evermore.

James Edward Seddon (1915–83)

34 *Go forth for God*

Magda   11 10 10 10

Ralph Vaughan Williams (1872–1958)

May also be sung to Woodlands (Nos. 125 or 136).

1 Go forth for God; go forth to the world in peace;
   be of good courage, armed with heavenly grace,
   in God's good Spirit daily to increase,
   till in his kingdom we behold his face.

2 Go forth for God; go forth to the world in strength;
   hold fast the good, be urgent for the right,
   render to no one evil; Christ at length
   shall overcome all darkness with his light.

3 Go forth for God; go forth to the world in love;
   strengthen the faint, give courage to the weak,
   help the afflicted; richly from above
   his love supplies the grace and power we seek.

4 Go forth for God; go forth to the world in joy,
   to serve God's people every day and hour,
   and serving Christ, our every gift employ,
   rejoicing in the Holy Spirit's power.

5 Sing praise to him who brought us on our way,
   sing praise to him who bought us with his blood,
   sing praise to him who sanctifies each day,
   sing praise to him who reigns one Lord and God.

John Raphael Peacey (1896–1971) and others

35 *Go, tell it on the mountain*

GO, TELL IT ON THE MOUNTAIN

North American traditional Spiritual
arr. Anthony F. Carver

REFRAIN *(Unison)*

Go, tell it on the moun - tain, o-ver the hills and ev-'ry-where.

Go, tell it on the moun - tain that Je - sus Christ is born.

Fine

VERSES *(Optional harmony)*

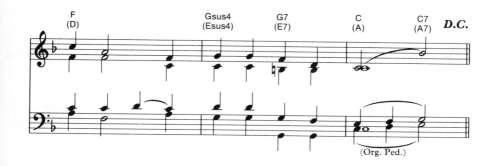

Go, tell it on the mountain,
over the hills and ev'rywhere.
Go, tell it on the mountain
that Jesus Christ is born.

1 While shepherds kept their watching
   o'er silent flocks by night,
   behold throughout the heavens
   there shone a holy light.

2 The shepherds feared and trembled
   when lo, above the earth
   rang out the angel chorus
   that hailed the Saviour's birth.

3 Down in a lowly manger
   our humble Christ was born;
   and God sent us salvation
   that blessèd Christmas morn.

North American traditional Spiritual

36 *Great is thy faithfulness*

FAITHFULNESS 11 10 11 10 with refrain   William Marion Runyan (1870–1957)

Broad and full

Great is thy faith-ful-ness! Great is thy faith-ful-ness! Morn-ing by

morn-ing new mer-cies I see; all I have need-ed thy

hand hath pro-vid-ed— great is thy faith-ful-ness, Lord, un-to me!

1 Great is thy faithfulness, O God my Father,
   there is no shadow of turning with thee;
   thou changest not, thy compassions they fail not,
   as thou hast been thou for ever wilt be.

   Great is thy faithfulness!
   Great is thy faithfulness!
   Morning by morning new mercies I see;
   all I have needed thy hand hath provided—
   great is thy faithfulness, Lord, unto me!

2 Summer and winter, and spring-time and harvest,
   sun, moon and stars in their courses above,
   join with all nature in manifold witness
   to thy great faithfulness, mercy and love.

3 Pardon for sin and a peace that endureth,
   thine own dear presence to cheer and to guide;
   strength for today and bright hope for tomorrow,
   blessings all mine, with ten thousand beside!

Thomas Obediah Chisholm (1866–1960)

37 *Have you heard the raindrops?*

RAINDROPS

Martin Christian Tinn Strover
(b. 1932)

There's wa - ter, wa-ter of life, Je - sus gives us the wa-ter of life: There's

68

wa - ter, wa-ter of life, Je - sus gives us the wa-ter of life.

1 Have you heard the raindrops drumming on the rooftops?
Have you heard the raindrops dripping on the ground?
Have you heard the raindrops splashing in the streams
and running to the rivers all around?

There's water, water of life,
Jesus gives us the water of life:
There's water, water of life,
Jesus gives us the water of life.

2 There's a busy workman digging in the desert,
digging with a spade that flashes in the sun:
soon there will be water rising in the wellshaft,
spilling from the bucket as it comes.

3 Nobody can live who hasn't any water,
when the land is dry then nothing much grows:
Jesus gives us life if we drink the living water,
sing it so that everybody knows.

Martin Christian Tinn Strover (b. 1932)

38 *Here from all nations*

O QUANTA QUALIA   11 10 11 10

Adaptation of a melody
from François de la Feillée's
Méthode du plainchant (1808)

For another harmonization of this tune see *Irish Church Hymnal* No. 441.

1 Here from all nations, all tongues, and all peoples,
   countless the crowd but their voices are one;
   vast is the sight and majestic their singing—
   'God has the victory: he reigns from the throne!'

2 These have come out of the hardest oppression;
   now they may stand in the presence of God,
   serving their Lord day and night in his temple,
   ransomed and cleansed by the Lamb's precious blood.

3 Gone is their thirst and no more shall they hunger,
   God is their shelter, his power at their side:
   sun shall not pain them, no burning will torture;
   Jesus the Lamb is their shepherd and guide.

4 He will go with them to clear living water
   flowing from springs which his mercy supplies:
   gone is their grief, and their trials are over;
   God wipes away every tear from their eyes.

5 Blessing and glory and wisdom and power
   be to the Saviour again and again;
   might and thanksgiving and honour for ever
   be to our God: Alleluia! Amen.

Christopher Martin Idle (b. 1938)
based on Revelation 7

39 *He is Lord*

HE IS LORD   6 11 10 6

Anon.
arr. Donald Davison

Rich and full

1 He is Lord, he is Lord;
   he is risen from the dead, and he is Lord;
   every knee shall bow, every tongue confess
   that Jesus Christ is Lord.

2 He is King, he is King;
   he will draw all nations to him, he is King;
   and the time shall be when the world shall sing
   that Jesus Christ is King.

3 He is love, he is love;
   he has shown us by his life that he is love;
   all his people sing with one voice of joy
   that Jesus Christ is love.

4 He is life, he is life;
   he has died to set us free and he is life;
   and he calls us all to live evermore,
   for Jesus Christ is life.

Anon.

40 *Holy Spirit, come, confirm us*

ALL FOR JESUS   87 87   John Stainer (1840–1901)

May also be sung to HALTON HOLGATE (No. 112).

1 Holy Spirit, come, confirm us
   in the truth that Christ makes known;
   we have faith and understanding
   through your helping gifts alone.

2 Holy Spirit, come, console us,
   come as advocate to plead,
   loving Spirit from the Father,
   grant in Christ the help we need.

3 Holy Spirit, come, renew us,
   come yourself to make us live,
   holy through your loving presence,
   holy through the gifts you give.

4 Holy Spirit, come, possess us,
   you the love of Three in One,
   Holy Spirit of the Father,
   Holy Spirit of the Son.

William Brian Foley (b. 1919)

41 *How beautiful the morning*

St Owen   10 13 10

Sherrell Prebble

With flowing simplicity

1 How beautiful the morning and the day;
my heart abounds with music, my lips can only say:
how beautiful the morning and the day.

2 How glorious the morning and the day;
my heart is still and listens, my soul begins to pray
to him who is the glory of the day.

3 How bountiful the blessings that he brings
of peace and joy and rapture that makes my spirit sing:
how bountiful the blessings that he brings.

4 How merciful the workings of his grace,
arousing faith and action my soul would never face
without his matchless mercy and his grace.

5 How barren was my life before he came,
supplying love and healing; I live now to acclaim
the majesty and wonder of his name.

Owen Barker

42 *How lovely on the mountains*

OUR GOD REIGNS

Leonard Smith Jnr.

How love-ly on the moun-tains are the feet of him who brings good news,_____ good news, an-noun-cing peace, pro-claim-ing news of hap-pi - ness:___ our God reigns,_____ our God reigns!

Verse 1 is the same in both versions. In the original version, rhythms need to be adjusted to fit the words.

POPULAR VERSION

1 How lovely on the mountains are the feet of him
  who brings good news, good news,
  announcing peace, proclaiming news of happiness:
  our God reigns, our God reigns!
    Our God reigns! (4 times)

2 You watchmen, lift your voices joyfully as one,
  shout for your king, your king.
  See eye to eye the Lord restoring Zion:
  your God reigns, your God reigns!
    Your God reigns! (4 times)

3 Waste places of Jerusalem, break forth with joy,
  we are redeemed, redeemed.
  The Lord has saved and comforted his people:
  your God reigns, your God reigns!

4 Ends of the earth, see the salvation of your God,
  Jesus is Lord, is Lord.
  Before the nations he has bared his holy arm:
  your God reigns, your God reigns!

(Original version overleaf)

77

1 How lovely on the mountains are the feet of him
who brings good news, good news,
announcing peace, proclaiming news of happiness:
our God reigns, our God reigns!
Our God reigns! (4 times)

2 He had no stately form, he had no majesty,
that we should be drawn to him.
He was despised and we took no account of him,
yet now he reigns with the most high.
Now he reigns (3 times)
with the most high!

3 It was our sin and guilt that bruised and wounded him,
it was our sin that brought him down.
When we like sheep had gone astray, our shepherd came
and on his shoulders bore our shame.
On his shoulders (3 times)
he bore our shame.

4 Meek as a lamb that's led out to the slaughterhouse,
dumb as a sheep before its shearer,
his life ran down upon the ground like pouring rain,
that we might be born again.
That we might be (3 times)
born again.

5 Out from the tomb he came with grace and majesty,
he is alive, he is alive.
God loves us so, see here his hands, his feet, his side,
yes, we know he is alive.
He is alive! (4 times)

6 How lovely on the mountains are the feet of him
who brings good news, good news,
announcing peace, proclaiming news of happiness:
our God reigns, our God reigns!
Our God reigns! (4 times)

Leonard Smith Jnr.

43 *I danced in the morning*
(Lord of the Dance)

LORD OF THE DANCE

Shaker tune adpt. Sydney Carter (b. 1915)
arr. John Birch

Lively and rhythmic

Unison

1. I danced in the morn-ing when the world was be-gun, and I danced in the moon and the stars__ and the sun, and I came down from heav-en and I danced on the earth; at Beth - le - hem I had my birth.

Refrain overleaf

REFRAIN

Dance then wher-ev-er you may be; I am the Lord of the
Dance, said he, and I'll lead you all, wher-ev-er you may be, and I'll

Straight on for vv. 2–5
lead you all in the dance, said he.

Last time
dance, said he.

VERSES 2–4

2. I danced for the scribe and the
3. I danced on the Sab-bath and I
4. I danced on a Fri-day when the

80

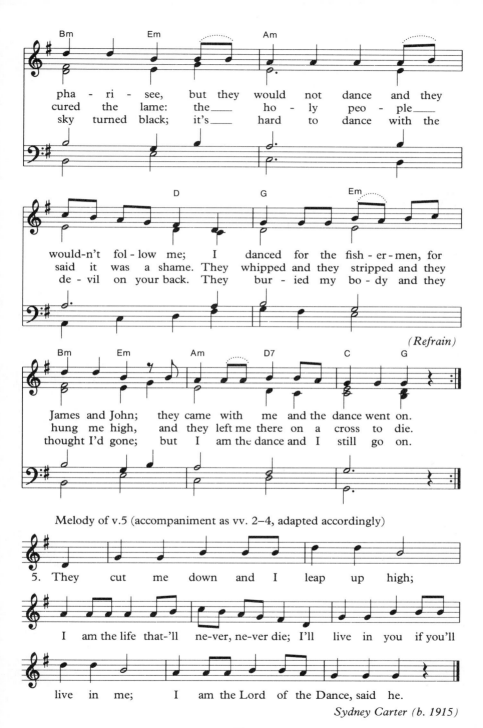

pha - ri - see, but they would not dance and they
cured the lame: the___ ho - ly peo - ple___
sky turned black; it's___ hard to dance with the

would-n't fol - low me; I danced for the fish - er - men, for
said it was a shame. They whipped and they stripped and they
de - vil on your back. They bur - ied my bo - dy and they

(Refrain)

James and John; they came with me and the dance went on.
hung me high, and they left me there on a cross to die.
thought I'd gone; but I am the dance and I still go on.

Melody of v.5 (accompaniment as vv. 2–4, adapted accordingly)

5. They cut me down and I leap up high;

I am the life that-'ll ne-ver, ne-ver die; I'll live in you if you'll

live in me; I am the Lord of the Dance, said he.

Sydney Carter (b. 1915)

81

44 *I sing a song of the saints of God*

GRAND ISLE

John Henry Hopkins (1861–1945)

1. I sing a song of the saints of God,
2. They loved their Lord so good and dear, and
3. They lived not on-ly in a - ges past, there are

pa - tient and brave and true, who toiled and fought and
his love made them strong; and they fol-lowed the right, for
hun-dreds of thou-sands still; the world is bright with the

lived and died for the Lord they loved and knew; and
Je - sus' sake, the whole of their good lives long; and
joy - ous saints who love to do Je - sus' will; you can

Music from *The Hymnal 1940*, The Church Pension Fund, New York.

one was a doc-tor, and one was a queen, and one was a shep-herd-ess
one was a sol-dier, and one was a priest, and one was slain by a
meet them in school, or in lanes, or at sea, in church, or in trains, or in

on the___ green: they were all of them saints of
fierce wild___ beast: and there's not a - ny rea - son,
shops, or at tea: for the saints of___ God are

God; and I mean, God help - ing, to be one too.
no, not the least, why I should-n't be one too.
just like___ me, and I mean to be one too.

Lesbia Scott (1898–1986)

83

45 *I will enter his gates*

I WILL ENTER

Leona von Brethorst

With pace and swing

Capo 3(C)

I will en-ter his gates___ with thanks-giv-ing in my heart; I will en-ter his courts with praise;___ I will say this is the day___ that the Lord has___ made; I will re-joice for he has made me

based on Psalm 118: 19, 24

85

46 Jesu, Jesu

CHEREPONI

Ghana folk-song
collected by Tom Colvin
arr. Anthony F. Carver

REFRAIN (Optional harmony)

Capo 2(D)

Gently

Je - su,_____ Je - su,_____ fill us with your love, show

us how to serve the neigh-bours we have from you._____

VERSES (Unison)

This song is effective and authentic if sung unaccompanied with improvised harmony
based mainly on parallel thirds and octaves. A hand-drum (e.g. bongos) might be used.

Jesu, Jesu,
fill us with your love,
show us how to serve
the neighbours we have from you.

1 Kneels at the feet of his friends,
  silently washes their feet,
  master who acts as a slave to them.

2 Neighbours are rich folk and poor,
  neighbours are black, brown and white,
  neighbours are nearby and far away.

3 These are the ones we should serve,
  these are the ones we should love.
  All these are neighbours to us and you.

4 Loving puts us on our knees,
  serving as though we were slaves,
  this is the way we should live with you.

Tom Colvin (c. 1965)
and the people of Ghana

47 *Led like a lamb*

LIKE A LAMB

Words and music by
Graham Kendrick (b. 1950)

Steady

INTRODUCTION

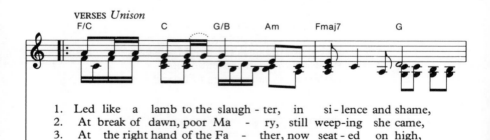

VERSES *Unison*

1. Led like a lamb to the slaugh-ter, in   si-lence and shame,
2. At break of dawn, poor Ma - ry, still weep-ing she came,
3. At the right hand of the Fa - ther, now seat-ed on high,

there on your back you car-ried a world of vio-lence and pain.
when through her grief she heard your voice now speak-ing her name.
you have be-gun your e-ter-nal_ reign of jus-tice and joy.

Bleed-ing,_ dy-ing,_
*Ma-ry!_ Mas-ter!_
Glo-ry,_ glo-ry,_

bleed-ing,_ dy-ing._
Ma-ry!_ Mas-ter!_
glo-ry,_ glo-ry._ *You're a -*

REFRAIN

*It is effective if the men sing 'Mary!' and the women reply 'Master!'

- live, you're a-live, you have ri-sen, *Al-le-lu-ia!* __

(al-le-lu-ia! al-le-lu-ia!)

And the

power and the glo-ry is gi-ven, *Al-le-lu-ia,* __

(al-le-lu-ia! al-le-lu-ia!)

Je-sus to

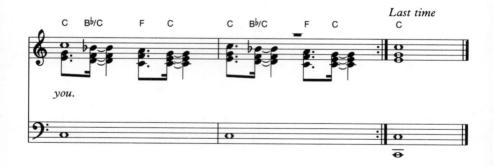

you.

*The word 'alleluia' can be sung antiphonally, as indicated, the people having been divided into three equal groups.

48 *Let every Christian pray*

LUDGATE 6 6 6 D

John Dykes Bower (1905–81)

May also be sung to LAUDES DOMINI (*Irish Church Hymnal* No. 400).

1 Let every Christian pray,
this day, and every day,
come, Holy Spirit, come.
Was not the Church we love
commissioned from above?
Come, Holy Spirit, come.

2 The Spirit brought to birth
the Church of Christ on earth
to seek and save the lost:
never has he withdrawn,
since that tremendous dawn,
his gifts at Pentecost.

3 Age after age, he strove
to teach her how to love:
come, Holy Spirit, come;
age after age, anew
she proved the gospel true:
come, Holy Spirit, come.

4 Only the Spirit's power
can fit us for this hour:
come, Holy Spirit, come;
instruct, inspire, unite;
and make us see the light:
come, Holy Spirit, come.

Frederick Pratt Green (b. 1903)

49 *Let there be love*

LET THERE BE LOVE   Dave Bilbrough

Triumphantly
Unison

Let there be love shared a-mong us, let there be love in our eyes, may now your love sweep this na-tion, cause us O Lord_____ to a - rise, give us a fresh un-der - stand-ing of bro-ther-ly love that is real, let there be

love shared a - mong us, let there be love.

Let there be love shared among us,
let there be love in our eyes,
may now your love sweep this nation,
cause us O Lord to arise,
give us a fresh understanding
of brotherly love that is real,
let there be love shared among us,
let there be love.

Dave Bilbrough

50 *Long ago, prophets knew*

PERSONENT HODIE 66 66 6 with refrain

Melody from *Piae Cantiones* (1582)
arr. Gustav Holst (1874–1934)

Ring, bells, ring,   ring,   ring!   Sing, choirs, sing,   sing,   sing!

For another setting of this tune see No. 31.

When he comes, when he comes, who will make him wel - come?
(4.) Je - sus comes, Je - sus comes: we will make him wel - come.

1 Long ago, prophets knew
Christ would come, born a Jew,
come to make all things new,
bear his people's burden,
freely love and pardon.

Ring, bells, ring, ring, ring!
Sing, choirs, sing, sing, sing!
When he comes,
when he comes,
who will make him welcome?

2 God in time, God in man,
this is God's timeless plan:
he will come, as a man,
born himself of woman,
God divinely human:

3 Mary hail! Though afraid,
she believed, she obeyed.
In her womb God is laid,
till the time expected,
nurtured and protected:

4 Journey ends: where afar
Bethlem shines, like a star,
stable door stands ajar.
Unborn Son of Mary,
Saviour, do not tarry.

Ring bells, ring, ring, ring!
Sing, choirs, sing, sing, sing!
Jesus comes,
Jesus comes:
we will make him welcome.

Frederick Pratt Green (b. 1903)

51 *Lord, for the years*

MARLBOROUGH PARK   11 10 11 10   William Donald Davison (b. 1937)

May also be sung to STRENGTH AND STAY (*Irish Church Hymnal* No. 174).

1 Lord, for the years your love has kept and guided,
   urged and inspired us, cheered us on our way;
   sought us and saved us, pardoned and provided,
   Lord of the years, we bring our thanks today.

2 Lord, for that word, the word of life which fires us,
   speaks to our hearts and sets our souls ablaze;
   teaches and trains, rebukes us and inspires us,
   Lord of the word, receive your people's praise.

3 Lord, for our land, in this our generation,
   spirits oppressed by pleasure, wealth and care;
   for young and old, for this and every nation,
   Lord of our land, be pleased to hear our prayer.

4 Lord, for our world, when we disown and doubt him,
   loveless in strength, and comfortless in pain;
   hungry and helpless, lost indeed without him,
   Lord of the world, we pray that Christ may reign.

5 Lord, for ourselves; in living power remake us—
   self on the cross and Christ upon the throne—
   past put behind us, for the future take us,
   Lord of our lives, to live for Christ alone.

Timothy Dudley-Smith (b. 1926)

52 Lord Jesus, we enthrone you

ENTHRONEMENT

Paul Gilbert Kyle (b. 1953)

Majestic

Lord Je-sus,___ we en-throne___ you,___ we pro-claim you our King.___ Stand-ing here___ in the midst of us___

we raise you up — with our praise,

and as we wor - ship build a throne,

and as we wor - ship build a throne,

and as we wor - ship build a throne, come Lord

Je - sus — and take your place.

Paul Gilbert Kyle (b. 1953), based on Psalm 22: 3

53 *Lord of all hopefulness*

Slane 10 11 11 12

Irish traditional melody
harm. Erik Reginald Routley (1917–82)

For another harmonization of this tune see No. 106.
For other variations of this tune (not suitable for singing to these words) see *Irish Church Hymnal* No. 322.

1 Lord of all hopefulness, Lord of all joy,
   whose trust, ever childlike, no cares could destroy,
   be there at our waking, and give us, we pray,
   your bliss in our hearts, Lord, at the break of the day.

2 Lord of all eagerness, Lord of all faith,
   whose strong hands were skilled at the plane and the lathe,
   be there at our labours, and give us, we pray,
   your strength in our hearts, Lord, at the noon of the day.

3 Lord of all kindliness, Lord of all grace,
   your hands swift to welcome, your arms to embrace,
   be there at our homing, and give us, we pray,
   your love in our hearts, Lord, at the eve of the day.

4 Lord of all gentleness, Lord of all calm,
   whose voice is contentment, whose presence is balm,
   be there at our sleeping, and give us, we pray,
   your peace in our hearts, Lord, at the end of the day.

Jan Struther (Joyce Placzek) (1901–53)

54 *Lord of the home*

WARRINGTON LM

Ralph Harrison (1748–1810)

For a slightly different harmonization of this tune (in B♭) see *Irish Church Hymnal* No. 258.

1 Lord of the home, your only Son
received a mother's tender love,
and from an earthly father won
his vision of your home above.

2 Help us, O Lord, our homes to make
your Holy Spirit's dwelling place;
our hands' and hearts' devotion take
to be the servants of your grace.

3 Teach us to keep our homes so fair
that, were our Lord a child once more,
he might be glad our hearth to share,
and find a welcome at our door.

4 Lord, may your Spirit sanctify
each household duty we fulfil;
may we our Master glorify
in glad obedience to your will.

Albert Frederick Bayly (1901–84)

55 *Lord, you were rich*

BERGERS   98 98 98

French traditional carol melody
arr. Donald Davison

1 Lord, you were rich beyond all splendour,
   yet, for love's sake, became so poor;
   leaving your throne in glad surrender,
   sapphire-paved courts for stable floor:
   Lord, you were rich beyond all splendour,
   yet, for love's sake, became so poor.

2 You are our God beyond all praising,
   yet, for love's sake, became a man
   stooping so low, but sinners raising
   heavenwards, by your eternal plan:
   you are our God, beyond all praising,
   yet, for love's sake, became a man.

3 Lord, you are love beyond all telling,
   Saviour and King, we worship you;
   Emmanuel, within us dwelling,
   make us and keep us pure and true:
   Lord, you are love beyond all telling,
   Saviour and King, we worship you.

Frank Houghton (1894–1972)
and in this version Jubilate Hymns

56 *Lord, the light of your love*
(Shine, Jesus, shine)

SHINE, JESUS, SHINE   Graham Kendrick (b. 1950)

Majestic and steady

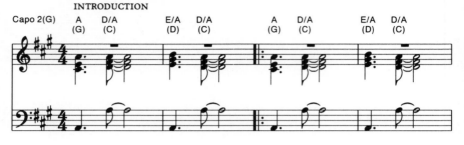

1. Lord, the light of your love is shin - ing in the midst of the
2. Lord, I come to your awe - some pres - ence, from the sha - dows in -
3. As we gaze on your king - ly bright - ness, so our fa - ces dis -

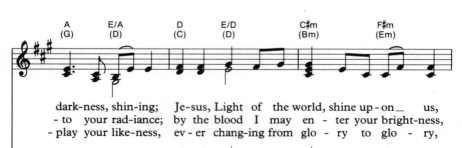

   dark-ness, shin-ing; Je-sus, Light of the world, shine up-on__ us,
   - to your rad-iance; by the blood I may en - ter your bright-ness,
   - play your like-ness, ev - er chang-ing from glo - ry to glo - ry,

set   us   free   by   the   truth   you   now   bring__ us,
search me,   try   me,   con - sume   all   my   dark - ness.
mir - rored here   may   our   lives   tell   your   sto -   ry.

shine   on____   me,   shine   on____   me.
Shine   on____   me,   shine   on____   me.
Shine   on____   me,   shine   on____   me.

REFRAIN

Shine,   Je - sus,   shine,___   fill   this   land   with   the

Fa - ther's   glo - ry;   blaze,   Spi - rit,   blaze,___   set   our

Graham Kendrick (b. 1950)
based on John 1: 1–5; 3: 19–21;
2 Corinthians 3: 18; 1 John 1: 7

57 *Make me a channel*

ST FRANCIS 8 10 10 8 with refrain

Sebastian Temple
arr. Donald Davison

Prayerfully, with gentle movement

1. Make me a chan-nel of your peace: where there is hat-red let me bring your
2. Make me a chan-nel of your peace: where there's des-pair in life let me bring
3. Make me a chan-nel of your peace: it is in par-don-ing that we are

Sebastian Temple
based on the Prayer of St Francis

58 *Meekness and majesty*

MEEKNESS AND MAJESTY

Majestically

Unison

Words and music by
Graham Kendrick (b. 1950)

1. Meek-ness and ma-jes-ty, man-hood and de-i-ty, in per-fect har-mo-ny, the man who is God.
2. Fa-ther's pure ra-di-ance, per-fect in in-no-cence, yet learns o-be-di-ence to death on a cross.
3. Wis-dom un-search-a-ble, God the in-vi-si-ble; love in-de-struc-ti-ble in frail-ty ap-pears.

Lord of e-ter-ni-ty dwells in hu-ma-ni-ty, kneels in hu-mi-li-ty and wash-es our feet.
Suf-fering to give us life, con-quering through sa-cri-fice; and as they cru-ci-fy prays 'Fa-ther, for-give.'
Lord of in-fi-ni-ty stoop-ing so ten-der-ly lifts our hu-ma-ni-ty to the heights of his throne.

based on John 3: 13–16, Philippians 2: 6–11

59 *Morning has broken*

BUNESSAN   55 54 D

Scots Gaelic traditional melody
arr. Donald Davison

For another setting of this tune see No. 11 or *Irish Church Hymnal* No. 56.

1 Morning has broken
like the first morning;
blackbird has spoken
like the first bird.
Praise for the singing!
Praise for the morning!
Praise for them, springing
fresh from the Word!

2 Sweet the rain's new fall
sunlit from heaven,
like the first dewfall
on the first grass.
Praise for the sweetness
of the wet garden,
sprung in completeness
where his feet pass.

3 Mine is the sunlight!
Mine is the morning
born of the one light
Eden saw play!
Praise with elation,
praise every morning,
God's re-creation
of the new day!

Eleanor Farjeon (1881–1965)

60 *May the mind of Christ my Saviour*

St Leonard's 87 85

Arthur Cyril Barham Gould (1891–1953)

1 May the mind of Christ my Saviour
live in me from day to day,
by his love and power controlling
all I do and say.

2 May the word of God enrich me
with his truth from hour to hour,
so that all may see I triumph
only through his power.

3 May the peace of God my Father
in my life for ever reign,
that I may be calm to comfort
those in grief and pain.

4 May the love of Jesus fill me
as the waters fill the sea,
him exalting, self abasing—
this is victory!

5 May his beauty rest upon me
as I seek to make him known;
so that all may look to Jesus,
seeing him alone.

6 May I run the race before me
strong and brave to face the foe,
looking only unto Jesus
as I onward go.

Katie Barclay Wilkinson (1859–1928), altd.

61 *Not for tongues of heaven's angels*

BRIDEGROOM   87 87 6

Peter Warwick Cutts (b. 1937)

1 Not for tongues of heaven's angels,
  not for wisdom to discern,
  not for faith that masters mountains,
  for this better gift we yearn:
  May love be ours, O Lord.

2 Love is humble, love is gentle,
  love is tender, true and kind;
  love is gracious, ever-patient,
  generous of heart and mind:
  May love be ours, O Lord.

3 Never jealous, never selfish,
  love will not rejoice in wrong;
  never boastful nor resentful,
  love believes and suffers long:
  May love be ours, O Lord.

4 In the day this world is fading
  faith and hope will play their part;
  but when Christ is seen in glory
  love shall reign in every heart:
  May love be ours, O Lord.

Timothy Dudley-Smith (b. 1926)
based on 1 Corinthians 13

62 *O Breath of life*

SPIRITUS VITAE 98 98 Mary Jane Hammond (1878–1964)

With sweeping breadth

May also be sung to ST CLEMENT (*Irish Church Hymnal* No. 32).

1 O Breath of life, come sweeping through us,
   revive your Church with life and power.
   O Breath of life, come, cleanse, renew us,
   and fit your Church to meet this hour.

2 O Wind of God, come, bend us, break us,
   till humbly we confess our need;
   then in your tenderness re-make us,
   revive, restore, for this we plead.

3 O Breath of love, come breathe within us,
   renewing thought and will and heart;
   come, love of Christ, afresh to win us,
   revive your Church in every part.

4 Revive us, Lord! Is zeal abating
   while harvest fields are vast and white?
   Revive us, Lord, the world is waiting,
   equip your Church to spread the light.

Elizabeth (Bessie) Ann Porter Head (1850–1936)

63 *O Christ, the healer*

DANIEL LM

Irish traditional melody
arr. Donald Davison

May also be sung to WAREHAM (*Irish Church Hymnal* No. 40).

1 O Christ, the healer, we have come
  to pray for health, to plead for friends.
  How can we fail to be restored
  when reached by love that never ends?

2 From every ailment flesh endures
  our bodies clamour to be freed;
  yet in our hearts we would confess
  that wholeness is our deepest need.

3 In conflicts that destroy our health
  we recognize the world's disease;
  our common life declares our ills.
  Is there no cure, O Christ, for these?

4 Grant that we all, made one in faith,
  in your community may find
  the wholeness that, enriching us,
  shall reach and prosper humankind.

Frederick Pratt Green (b. 1903)

64 O Christ the same

LONDONDERRY AIR 11 10 11 10 11 10 11 12

Irish traditional melody
arr. Donald Davison

Unison

1. O Christ the same, through all our sto-ry's pa - ges, our loves and hopes, our fail-ures and our fears;___ e-ter-nal Lord, the King of all the a - ges,___ un-chang-ing still, a-mid the pass-ing years –___ O liv-ing Word, the source of all cre - a - tion,___ who spread the skies, and set the stars a -

- blaze,_____ O Christ the same, who wrought our whole sal - va - tion,_____ we bring our thanks to you for all our yes-ter - days.

1 O Christ the same, through all our story's pages,
   our loves and hopes, our failures and our fears;
   eternal Lord, the King of all the ages,
   unchanging still, amid the passing years—
   O living Word, the source of all creation,
   who spread the skies, and set the stars ablaze,
   O Christ the same, who wrought our whole salvation,
   we bring our thanks to you for all our yesterdays.

2 O Christ the same, the friend of sinners sharing
   our inmost thoughts, the secrets none can hide,
   still as of old upon your body bearing
   the marks of love, in triumph glorified—
   O Son of Man, who stooped for us from heaven,
   O Prince of life, in all your saving power,
   O Christ the same, to whom our hearts are given,
   we bring our thanks to you for this the present hour.

3 O Christ the same, secure within whose keeping
   our lives and loves, our days and years remain,
   our work and rest, our waking and our sleeping,
   our calm and storm, our pleasure and our pain—
   O Lord of love, for all our joys and sorrows,
   for all our hopes, when earth shall fade and flee,
   O Christ the same, beyond our brief tomorrows,
   we bring our thanks to you for all that is to be.

Timothy Dudley-Smith (b. 1926)
based on Hebrews 13: 8

65   O let us spread the pollen of peace

THE POLLEN OF PEACE

Roger Brian Courtney (b. 1954)
arr. Norman Lloyd Richardson (b. 1947)

O let us__ spread the pol-len of peace__ through-out our

land,_____ let us spread the pol-len of peace through-out our

land._____ Let us spread the pol-len of peace,__ and

make all hat - red cease; let us spread the pol-len of peace

VERSES *(Unison)*

1. Oh Christ_ has sown the seeds of love;_
2. All it needs is our love to make it grow;_

_____ Christ_ has launched the wing-èd
_ all it needs is our hope-ful-ness to

throughout our land.____ land.____

124

Roger Brian Courtney (b. 1954)
Written for the Corrymeela Community

66 · *O Lord my God!*
(How great thou art!)

How Great Thou Art   11 10 11 10 10 8 10 8

Russian hymn-tune
arr. Stuart K. Hine (b. 1899)

Majestically

REFRAIN

Then sings my   soul,   my Sav-iour God, to   thee,   How great thou

art! *How great thou art!* *Then sings my soul, my Sav-iour God, to*

thee, *How great thou* *art! ___ How great_ thou_ art!*

1 O Lord my God! When I in awesome wonder
consider all the works thy hand hath made,
I see the stars, I hear the mighty thunder,
thy pow'r throughout the universe display'd:

Then sings my soul, my Saviour God, to thee,
How great thou art! How great thou art!
Then sings my soul, my Saviour God, to thee,
How great thou art! How great thou art!

2 When through the woods and forest glades I wander,
and hear the birds sing sweetly in the trees;
when I look down from lofty mountain grandeur,
and hear the brook, and feel the gentle breeze:

3 And when I think that God his Son not sparing,
sent him to die—I scarce can take it in.
That on the cross my burden gladly bearing,
he bled and died to take away my sin:

4 When Christ shall come with shout of acclamation
and take me home—what joy shall fill my heart!
Then I shall bow in humble adoration
and there proclaim, my God, how great thou art!

Russian hymn, tr. Stuart K. Hine (b. 1899)
based on Psalm 8; Romans 5: 9–11;
1 Thessalonians 4: 16–17

67 *O Lord of creation*

PETRIE'S CROWN   11 11 11 11

Irish traditional melody
arr. Donald Davison

May also be sung to SLANE (Nos. 53 or 106) by omitting the word 'O' at the beginning of each verse.

1 O Lord of creation, to you be all praise!
Most mighty your working, most wondrous your ways!
Your glory and might are beyond us to tell,
and yet in the heart of the humble you dwell.

2 O Lord of all power, I give you my will,
in joyful obedience your tasks to fulfil.
Your bondage is freedom; your service is song;
and, held in your keeping, my weakness is strong.

3 O Lord of all wisdom, I give you my mind,
rich truth that surpasses our knowledge to find;
what eye has not seen and what ear has not heard
is taught by your Spirit and shines from your Word.

4 O Lord of all bounty, I give you my heart;
I praise and adore you for all you impart,
your love to inspire me, your counsel to guide,
your presence to shield me, whatever betide.

5 O Lord of all being, I give you my all;
if I ever disown you, I stumble and fall;
but, led in your service your word to obey,
I'll walk in your freedom to the end of the way.

Jack Copley Winslow (1882–1974), altd.

68 _O Lord of every shining constellation_

KERRINGTON   11 10 11 10   William Donald Davison (b. 1937)

With breadth
Unison

May also be sung to HIGHWOOD or STRENGTH AND STAY (_Irish Church Hymnal_ Nos. 420 and 25).

1 O Lord of every shining constellation
   that wheels in splendour through the midnight sky:
   grant us your Spirit's true illumination
   to read the secrets of your work on high.

2 You, Lord, have made the atom's hidden forces;
   your laws its mighty energies fulfil:
   teach us, to whom you give such rich resources,
   in all we use, to serve your holy will.

3 O Life, awaking life in cell and tissue;
   from flower to bird, from beast to brain of man:
   help us to trace, from birth to final issue,
   the sure unfolding of your ageless plan.

4 You, Lord, have stamped your image on your creatures
   and, though they mar that image, love them still:
   lift up our eyes to Christ, that in his features
   we may discern the beauty of your will.

5 Great Lord of nature, shaping and renewing,
   you made us more than nature's sons to be;
   you help us tread, with grace our souls enduing,
   the road to life and immortality.

Albert Frederick Bayly (1901–84)

69 *O sing a song of Bethlehem*

Kingsfold DCM

English traditional melody
arr. Ralph Vaughan Williams (1872–1958)

May also be sung to Forest Green (*Irish Church Hymnal* No. 66).

1 O sing a song of Bethlehem,
   of shepherds watching there,
   and of the news that came to them
   from angels in the air:
   the light that shone on Bethlehem
   fills all the world today;
   of Jesus' birth and peace on earth
   the angels sing alway.

2 O sing a song of Nazareth,
   of sunny days of joy,
   O sing of fragrant flowers' breath
   and of the sinless boy:
   for now the flowers of Nazareth
   in every heart may grow;
   now spreads the fame of his dear name
   on all the winds that blow.

3 O sing a song of Galilee,
   of lake and woods and hill,
   of him who walked upon the sea
   and bade its waves be still:
   for though, like waves on Galilee,
   dark seas of trouble roll,
   when faith has heard the Master's word,
   falls peace upon the soul.

4 O sing a song of Calvary,
   its glory and dismay;
   of him who hung upon the tree,
   and took our sins away:
   for he who died on Calvary
   is risen from the grave,
   and Christ our Lord, by heaven adored,
   is mighty now to save.

Louis Fitzgerald Benson (1855–1930)

70 One more step along the world I go

SOUTHCOTE 99 79 with refrain

Sydney Carter (b. 1915)
arr. Donald Davison

And it's from the old I tra-vel to the new; keep me tra-vel-ling a-long with you.

1 One more step along the world I go,
 one more step along the world I go:
 from the old things to the new
 keep me travelling along with you:

 And it's from the old I travel to the new;
 keep me travelling along with you.

2 Round the corner of the world I turn,
 more and more about the world I learn;
 all the new things that I see
 you'll be looking at along with me:

3 As I travel through the bad and good,
 keep me travelling the way I should;
 where I see no way to go
 you'll be telling me the way, I know:

4 Give me courage when the world is rough,
 keep me loving though the world is tough;
 leap and sing in all I do,
 keep me travelling along with you:

5 You are older than the world can be,
 you are younger than the life in me;
 ever old and ever new,
 keep me travelling along with you:

Sydney Carter (b. 1915)

71 *O Lord, the clouds are gathering*

GATHERING CLOUDS

Graham Kendrick (b. 1950)

With strength

Unison

1. O — Lord, — the clouds are gath - er - ing, the fire of judge-ment
(2.) Lord, — o - ver the na - tions now where is the dove of
(3.) Lord, — dark powers are poised to flood our streets with hate and
(4.) Lord, — your glo - rious cross shall tower tri - um - phant in this

burns, — how we have fal - len! O —
peace? — Her wings are bro - ken. O —
fear; — we must a - wa - ken! O —
land, — e - vil con - found - ing. Through the

Lord, — you stand ap - pall'd to see your laws of love so
Lord, — while pre-cious child - ren starve the tools of war in -
Lord, — let love re - claim the lives that sin would sweep a -
fire — your suff-'ring Church dis-play the glo - ries of her

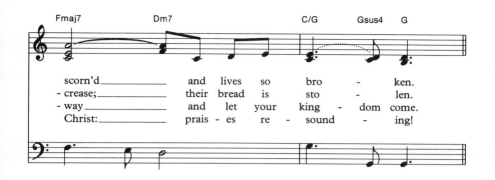

scorn'd_____ and lives so bro - ken.
- crease;_____ their bread is sto - len.
- way_____ and let your king - dom come.
Christ:_____ prais - es re - sound - ing!

REFRAIN

(Women)

Have mer - cy, Lord,_____ for - give us, Lord,__ re -

(Men)

Have mer - cy, Lord,_____ for - give us, Lord,_____ re -

- store us, Lord, re-vive your Church a - gain._____

- store us, Lord, re-vive your Church a - gain._____ Let

Let jus-tice flow___ like ri - vers__ and

jus - tice flow___ like ri - vers___ and

right - eous-ness like a ne - ver fail - ing stream.

right - eous-ness like a ne - ver fail - ing stream.

2. O___ a ne-ver fail-ing stream.___
3. O___
4. Yet, O

Graham Kendrick (b. 1950)
based on Isaiah 58: 6–9; Amos 5: 24

72 *Promised Lord*

PROMISED LORD   7 7 with refrain

American traditional melody
arr. Donald Davison

Come, O — Lord, — quick-ly — come. — Come in glo - ry, —

come in — glo - ry, come in — glo - ry, quick-ly — come.

1 Promised Lord and Christ is he,
   May we soon his kingdom see.

   Come, O Lord, quickly come.
   Come in glory,
   come in glory,
   come in glory,
   quickly come.

2 Teaching, healing, once was he.
   May we soon his kingdom see.

3 Dead and buried once was he.
   May we soon his kingdom see.

4 Risen from the dead is he.
   May we soon his kingdom see.

5 Soon to come again is he.
   May we soon his kingdom see.

Roger Ruston

73 Rise and hear!

SUSSEX 87 87

English traditional melody
adpt. Ralph Vaughan Williams (1872–1958)

1 Rise and hear! The Lord is speaking,
as the gospel words unfold;
we, in all our agelong seeking,
find no firmer truth to hold.

2 Word of goodness, truth, and beauty,
heard by simple folk and wise,
word of freedom, word of duty,
word of life beyond our eyes.

3 Word of God's forgiveness granted
to the wild or guilty soul,
word of love that works undaunted,
changes, heals, and makes us whole.

4 Speak to us, O Lord, believing,
as we hear, the sower sows;
may our hearts, your word receiving,
be the good ground where it grows.

Howard Charles Adie Gaunt (1902–83)

74 *Rejoice!*

REJOICE   Graham Kendrick (b. 1950)

Re - joice! Re-joice! Christ is in you, the hope of glo - ry in our hearts. He lives! He lives! His breath is in you, a - rise a migh - ty ar - my, we a - rise.

continued overleaf

VERSES

1. Now is the time for us to march u-pon the land, into our hands he will give the ground we claim.

He rides in ma-jes-ty to lead us in-to vic-to-ry, the world shall see that Christ is Lord! *Re*-

(Refrain)

142

Rejoice! Rejoice! Christ is in you,
the hope of glory in our hearts.
He lives! He lives! His breath is in you,
arise a mighty army, we arise.

1 Now is the time for us
   to march upon the land,
   into our hands
   he will give the ground we claim.
   He rides in majesty
   to lead us into victory,
   the world shall see
   that Christ is Lord!

2 God is at work in us
   his purpose to perform,
   building a kingdom
   of power not of words,
   where things impossible
   by faith shall be made possible;
   let's give the glory
   to him now.

3 Though we are weak, his grace
   is everything we need;
   we're made of clay
   but this treasure is within.
   He turns our weaknesses
   into his opportunities,
   so that the glory
   goes to him.

Graham Kendrick (b. 1950)
based on 1 Corinthians 4: 20;
2 Corinthians 4: 7; 12: 10; Colossians 1: 27

75 Safe in the shadow

CREATOR GOD   CM

Norman Leonard Warren (b. 1934)

1 Safe in the shadow of the Lord
  beneath his hand and power,
  I trust in him,
  I trust in him,
  my fortress and my tower.

2 My hope is set on God alone
  though Satan spreads his snare,
  I trust in him,
  I trust in him,
  to keep me in his care.

3 From fears and phantoms of the night,
  from foes about my way,
  I trust in him,
  I trust in him,
  by darkness as by day.

4 His holy angels keep my feet
  secure from every stone;
  I trust in him,
  I trust in him,
  and unafraid go on.

5 Strong in the Everlasting Name,
  and in my Father's care,
  I trust in him,
  I trust in him,
  who hears and answers prayer.

6 Safe in the shadow of the Lord,
  possessed by love divine,
  I trust in him,
  I trust in him,
  and meet his love with mine.

Timothy Dudley-Smith (b. 1926)
based on Psalm 91

76 *Seek, O seek the Lord*

Venantius 77 75 with refrain

Richard Connolly (b. 1927)

Seek, O seek the Lord, while he is near; trust him, speak to him in prayer, and he will hear.

A cantor or small group may sing first the refrain, and then each verse, the congregation responding with the refrain in each case.

146

Seek, O seek the Lord, while he is near;
trust him, speak to him in prayer,
and he will hear.

1 God be with us in our lives,
   direct us in our calling;
   break the snares the world contrives,
   keep us from falling.

2 God, increase in us the life
   that Christ by dying gave us:
   though we faint in mortal strife
   his blood will save us.

3 Strengthen in our hearts the love
   we owe to one another;
   how can we love God above
   and not our brother?

James Phillip McAuley (1917–76)
based on Isaiah 55

77 Seek ye first

SEEK YE FIRST

Karen Lafferty

The *Alleluia* refrain is sung by soprano voices while the others repeat the verse.

1 Seek ye first the kingdom of God,
and his righteousness,
and all these things shall be added unto you;
Allelu-, alleluia:

   Alleluia, alleluia, alleluia, alleluia!

2 Ask, and it shall be given unto you;
seek, and ye shall find;
knock, and the door shall be opened unto you;
Allelu-, alleluia:

3 Man shall not live by bread alone,
but by every word
that proceeds from the mouth of the Lord;
Allelu-, alleluia:

Karen Lafferty
based on Matthew 6: 33 and 7: 7,
and Deuteronomy 8: 3

78 *Set your troubled hearts at rest*

LYNCH'S LULLABY   77 77 D

Irish cradle song
from J. P. Lynch's *Melodies of Ireland* (c.1845)
arr. Donald Davison

Calmly

This tune covers two verses at a time.
May also be sung to SONG 13 (*Irish Church Hymnal* No. 580).

150

1 'Set your troubled hearts at rest'—
  hear again the word divine;
  all our Father does is best;
  let his peace be yours and mine.

2 Trusting still in God above,
  set your troubled hearts at rest;
  find within a Father's love
  comfort for a soul distressed.

3 When you come to make request
  know that God will answer prayer;
  set your troubled hearts at rest,
  safe within a Father's care.

4 Be at peace, then, and rejoice,
  loved and comforted and blessed;
  hear again the Saviour's voice:
  'Set your troubled hearts at rest.'

Timothy Dudley-Smith (b. 1926)
based on John 14: 1

79 *Spirit of God*

SKYE BOAT SONG   CM with refrain

Scottish folk-song
arr. Donald Davison

With gentle movement

Spi - rit of God, un -seen as the wind, gen - tle as is the dove; teach us the truth and help us be-lieve, show us the Sav - iour's love.

May be sung unaccompanied.

152

*Alternatively the melody may remain on E throughout this bar.

Spirit of God, unseen as the wind,
gentle as is the dove;
teach us the truth and help us believe,
show us the Saviour's love.

1 You spoke to us long, long ago,
   gave us the written word;
   we read it still, needing its truth,
   through it God's voice is heard.

2 Without your help we fail our Lord,
   we cannot live his way;
   we need your power, we need your strength,
   following Christ each day.

Margaret Old (b. 1932)

80 *Thanks to God*

Kingley Vale   87 87 47   Hugh Percy Allen (1869–1946)

May also be sung to Regent Square (*Irish Church Hymnal* No. 234), repeating the penultimate line of each verse.

1 Thanks to God whose Word was spoken
in the deed that made the earth.
His the voice that called a nation,
his the fires that tried her worth.
God has spoken:
praise him for his open Word.

2 Thanks to God whose Word incarnate
glorified the flesh of man.
Deeds and words and death and rising
tell the grace in heaven's plan.
God has spoken:
praise him for his open Word.

3 Thanks to God whose Word was written
in the Bible's sacred page,
record of the revelation
showing God to every age.
God has spoken:
praise him for his open Word.

4 Thanks to God whose Word is published
in the tongues of every race.
See its glory undiminished
by the change of time or place.
God has spoken:
praise him for his open Word.

5 Thanks to God whose Word is answered
by the Spirit's voice within.
Here we drink of joy unmeasured,
life redeemed from death and sin.
God is speaking:
praise him for his open Word.

Reginald Thomas Brooks (1918–85)

81 *The King is among us*

THE KING IS AMONG US 65 65

Graham Kendrick (b. 1950)

1. The King is a-mong us, his Spi-rit is here; let's draw near and wor - - - ship, let songs fill the air.

2. He

*The first note of this bar should be sung lightly, rather as if the bar-line were placed after it.

1 The King is among us,
  his Spirit is here;
  let's draw near and worship,
  let songs fill the air.

2 He looks down upon us,
  delight in his face,
  enjoying his children's love,
  enthralled by our praise.

3 For each child is special,
  accepted and loved,
  a love gift from Jesus
  to his Father above.

4 And now he is giving
  his gifts to us all,
  for no one is worthless
  and each one is called.

5 The Spirit's anointing
  on all flesh comes down,
  and we shall be channels
  for works like his own.

6 We come now believing
  your promise of power,
  for we are your people
  and this is your hour.

7 The King is among us,
  his Spirit is here;
  let's draw near and worship,
  let songs fill the air.

Graham Kendrick (b. 1950)

82 *The light of Christ*

THE LIGHT OF CHRIST

Donald Fishel (b. 1928)
arr. Anthony F. Carver

Flowing

REFRAIN*

The light of Christ has come into the world; the light of Christ has come.

The light of Christ has come into the world; the light of Christ has come into the world;

*The congregation should be encouraged to sing the refrain in two parts. The parts may be exchanged, or sung by a mixture of high and low voices, as desired.

VERSES *Unison*

1. We must all be__ born a - gain to__
2. God gave up his__ on - ly Son out of
3. The light of Christ has__ come to us so that

see the king-dom of God; the__ wa - ter and the
love__ for the world, so that all__ who be -
we might have sal - va - tion; from the dark-ness of our

Spi - rit bring new life__ in God's love._____
- lieve in him will_ live__ for__ ev - er._____
sins we walk in-to glo - ry with Christ Je - sus._____

D.C.

v.1 *

**v.3*

Donald Fishel (b. 1928), based on John 3

159

83 *The sinless one to Jordan came*

PUER NOBIS NASCITUR LM

Melody adpt. Michael Praetorius (1571–1621)
harm. George Ratcliffe Woodward (1848–1934)

For an alternative harmonization of this tune see *Irish Church Hymnal* No. 82.
May also be sung to SOLEMNIS HAEC FESTIVITAS (*Irish Church Hymnal* No. 175).

The Baptism of Christ
(suitable also for Adult Baptism and Confirmation)

1 The sinless one to Jordan came
   to share our fallen nature's blame;
   God's righteousness he thus fulfilled
   and chose the path his Father willed.

2 Uprising from the waters there,
   the voice from heaven did witness bear
   that he, the Son of God, had come
   to lead his scattered people home.

3 Above him see the heavenly Dove,
   the sign of God the Father's love,
   now by the Holy Spirit shed
   upon the Son's anointed head.

4 How blest that mission then begun
   to heal and save a race undone;
   straight to the wilderness he goes
   to wrestle with his people's foes.

5 Dear Lord, let those baptized from sin
   go forth with you, a world to win;
   and send the Holy Spirit's power
   to shield them in temptation's hour.

6 On you shall all your people feed
   and know you are the Bread indeed,
   who gives eternal life to those
   that with you died, and with you rose.

George Boorne Timms (b. 1910)

84 *The Spirit came, as promised*

DAY OF REST   76 76 D

James William Elliott (1833–1915)

This tune may be used for 'O Jesus, I have promised' (*Irish Church Hymnal* No. 544) and MISSIONARY, the set tune there, may be sung to the text here.

1 The Spirit came, as promised,
   in God's appointed hour;
   and now to each believer
   he comes in love and power:
   and by his Holy Spirit
   God seals us as his own,
   and through his Son and Spirit
   makes access to his throne.

2 The Spirit makes our bodies
   the temple of the Lord;
   he binds us all together
   in faith and true accord:
   the Spirit in his greatness
   brings power from God above
   and with the Son and Father
   dwells in our hearts in love.

3 He bids us live together
   in unity and peace,
   employ his gifts in blessing
   and let base passions cease:
   we should not grieve the Spirit
   by open sin or shame,
   nor let our words and actions
   deny his holy name.

4 The word, the Spirit's weapon,
   will bring all sin to light;
   and prayer, by his directing,
   will add new joy and might:
   be filled then with his Spirit,
   live out God's will and word;
   rejoice with hymns and singing,
   make music to the Lord!

James Edward Seddon (1915–83)

85 *The voice of God*

MORESTEAD   10 10 10 10   Sydney Watson (b. 1903)

May also be sung to WOODLANDS (Nos. 125 or 136).

1 The voice of God goes out to all the world;
  his glory speaks across the universe.
  The great King's herald cries from star to star:
  with power, with justice, he will walk his way.

2 The Lord has said: 'Receive my messenger,
  my promise to the world, my pledge made flesh,
  a lamp to every nation, light from light':
  with power, with justice, he will walk his way.

3 The broken reed he will not trample down,
  nor set his heel upon the dying flame.
  He binds the wounds, and health is in his hand:
  with power, with justice, he will walk his way.

4 Anointed with the Spirit and with power,
  he comes to crown with comfort all the weak,
  to show the face of justice to the poor:
  with power, with justice, he will walk his way.

5 His touch will bless the eyes that darkness held,
  the lame shall run, the halting tongue shall sing,
  and prisoners laugh in light and liberty:
  with power, with justice, he will walk his way.

Peter Icarus

86 *There is a Redeemer*

THERE IS A REDEEMER

Melody Green

Hymn-like
Unison

Capo 2(D)

1. There is a Re-deem - er, Je - sus, God's own

Son, _____ pre - cious Lamb of

God, Mes-si-ah, Ho - - ly One.

REFRAIN

Thank you, O my Fa - ther, for giv-ing us your

1 There is a Redeemer,
  Jesus, God's own Son,
  precious Lamb of God, Messiah,
  Holy One.

   Thank you, O my Father,
   for giving us your Son,
   and leaving your Spirit
   till the work on earth is done.

2 Jesus my Redeemer,
  Name above all names,
  precious Lamb of God, Messiah,
  O for sinners slain.

3 When I stand in glory
  I will see his face,
  and there I'll serve my King for ever,
  in that holy place.

Melody Green
based on Isaiah 47: 4; Acts 1: 8;
Philippians 2: 9; Revelation 22: 3–4

87 *There is singing in the desert*

BATTLE HYMN

William Steffe (c.1852)
arr. Donald Davison

At a moderate marching pace

Come and sing a-loud your prais - es,___

This tune can also be sung to the words 'Mine eyes have seen the glory' (*Irish Church Hymnal* No. 424), the (optional) refrain being 'Glory, glory, alleluia' (3 times) followed by the last line of the preceding verse.

come and sing a-loud your prais - es, come and sing a-loud your prais - es, for Je - sus Christ__ is here.

1 There is singing in the desert, there is laughter in the skies,
   there are wise men filled with wonder, there are shepherds with surprise,
   you can tell the world is dancing by the light that's in their eyes,
   for Jesus Christ is here.

   Come and sing aloud your praises,
   come and sing aloud your praises,
   come and sing aloud your praises,
   for Jesus Christ is here.

2 He hears deaf men by the lakeside, he sees blind men in the streets,
   he goes up to those who cannot walk, he talks to all he meets,
   touching silken robes or tattered clothes, it's everyone he greets,
   for Jesus Christ is here.

Geoffrey Marshall-Taylor (b. 1943)

88 *There's a spirit in the air*

LAUDS 77 77   John Whitridge Wilson (b. 1905)

DESCANT (*v.7 – optional*)

Praise___ the love!___ Praise___ the love!___ Al – – le - lu - ia! Al – – – le - lu - ia!___

Small notes are for organ only.
May also be sung to ORIENTIS PARTIBUS (*Irish Church Hymnal* No. 625).

1 There's a spirit in the air,
 telling Christians everywhere:
 'Praise the love that Christ revealed,
 living, working, in our world.'

2 Lose your shyness, find your tongue,
 tell the world what God has done:
 God in Christ has come to stay.
 Live tomorrow's life today!

3 When believers break the bread,
 when a hungry child is fed,
 praise the love that Christ revealed,
 living, working, in our world.

4 Still his Spirit gives us light,
 seeing wrong and setting right:
 God in Christ has come to stay.
 Live tomorrow's life today!

5 When a stranger's not alone,
 where the homeless find a home,
 praise the love that Christ revealed,
 living, working, in our world.

6 May the Spirit fill our praise,
 guide our thoughts and change our ways.
 God in Christ has come to stay.
 Live tomorrow's life today!

7 There's a Spirit in the air,
 calling people everywhere:
 praise the love that Christ revealed,
 living, working, in our world.

Brian Arthur Wren (b. 1936)

89 *Thine be the glory*

MACCABAEUS   10 11 11 11 with refrain   George Frideric Handel (1685–1759)

Thine be the glo - ry, ri - sen,_ con-quering Son, end - less_ is the vic - tory thou o'er death hast won.

1 Thine be the glory, risen, conquering Son,
endless is the victory thou o'er death hast won;
angels in bright raiment rolled the stone away,
kept the folded grave-clothes where thy body lay:

   Thine be the glory, risen, conquering Son,
   endless is the victory thou o'er death hast won.

2 Lo, Jesus meets us, risen from the tomb;
lovingly he greets us, scatters fear and gloom;
let the Church with gladness hymns of triumph sing,
for her Lord now liveth, death hath lost its sting:

3 No more we doubt thee, glorious Prince of Life;
life is nought without thee: aid us in our strife;
make us more than conquerors through thy deathless love;
bring us safe through Jordan to thy home above:

   Edmond Louis Budry (1854–1932)
   tr. Richard Birch Hoyle (1875–1939)

90 *This is my will*

Emly   44 44 44 44

Irish traditional melody
arr. Donald Davison

1 'This is my will,
  my one command,
  that love should dwell
  among you all.
  This is my will,
  that you should love
  as I have shown
  that I love you.

2 No greater love
  can be than this:
  to choose to die
  to save one's friends.
  You are my friends
  if you obey
  what I command
  that you should do.

3 I call you now
  no longer slaves;
  no slave knows all
  his master does.
  I call you friends,
  for all I hear
  my Father say
  you hear from me.

4 You chose not me,
  but I chose you,
  that you should go
  and bear much fruit.
  I chose you out
  that you in me
  should bear much fruit
  that will abide.

5 All that you ask
  my Father dear
  for my name's sake
  you shall receive.
  This is my will,
  my one command,
  that love should dwell
  in each, in all.'

James Quinn (b. 1919)
based on John 15: 12–17

91 *This is the day*

THIS IS THE DAY

Fiji Island folk-melody
arr. Anthony F. Carver

Joyfully, with bounce
Unison

1. This is the day, this is the day that the Lord has made, that the

Lord has made. We will re-joice, we will re-joice and be

glad in it, and be glad in it. This is the day that the

Lord has made. We will re-joice and be glad in___ it.

This is the day, this is the day that the Lord has made.

1 This is the day that the Lord has made.
   We will rejoice and be glad in it.

2 This is the day when he rose again.
   We will rejoice and be glad in it.

3 This is the day when the Spirit came.
   We will rejoice and be glad in it.

based on Psalm 118: 24

92 *To God be the glory!*

To God Be The Glory   11 11 11 11 with refrain

William Howard Doane
(1832–1915)

Praise the Lord! Praise the Lord! Let the earth hear his voice! Praise the

This tune is frequently sung with dotted quaver rhythm throughout.

Lord! Praise the Lord! Let the peo-ple re - joice!

O come__ to the Fa-ther, through Je-sus the Son: and

give him the glo - ry! Great things he hath done!

1 To God be the glory! Great things he hath done!
  So loved he the world that he gave us his Son;
  who yielded his life an atonement for sin,
  and opened the life gate that all may go in.

  Praise the Lord! Praise the Lord! Let the earth hear his voice!
  Praise the Lord! Praise the Lord! Let the people rejoice!
  O come to the Father, through Jesus the Son:
  and give him the glory! Great things he hath done!

2 O perfect redemption, the purchase of blood!
  To every believer the promise of God;
  the vilest offender who truly believes,
  that moment from Jesus a pardon receives.

3 Great things he hath taught us, great things he hath done,
  and great our rejoicing through Jesus the Son;
  but purer, and higher, and greater will be
  our wonder, our rapture, when Jesus we see.

Frances van Alstyne (1820–1915)

179

93 We have a gospel

FULDA LM

William Gardiner,
Sacred Melodies (1815)

For a variation of this tune (not suitable for singing to these words), see *Irish Church Hymnal* No. 37.

1 We have a gospel to proclaim,
   good news for all throughout the earth;
   the gospel of a Saviour's name:
   we sing his glory, tell his worth.

2 Tell of his birth at Bethlehem,
   not in a royal house or hall
   but in a stable dark and dim:
   the Word made flesh, a light for all.

3 Tell of his death at Calvary,
   hated by those he came to save;
   in lonely suffering on the cross
   for all he loved, his life he gave.

4 Tell of that glorious Easter morn:
   empty the tomb, for he was free;
   he broke the power of death and hell
   that we might share his victory.

5 Tell of his reign at God's right hand,
   by all creation glorified;
   he sends his Spirit on his Church
   to live for him, the Lamb who died.

6 Now we rejoice to name him King;
   Jesus is Lord of all the earth:
   this gospel-message we proclaim,
   we sing his glory, tell his worth.

Edward Joseph Burns (b. 1938)

94 *We turn to Christ anew*

LEONI   66 84 D

Adapted from a Synagogue melody
by Meyer Lyon (1751–97)
and Thomas Olivers (1725–99)

For an alternative harmonization see *Irish Church Hymnal* No. 332.

1 We turn to Christ anew
who hear his call today,
his way to walk, his will pursue,
his word obey.
To serve him as our king
and of his kingdom learn,
from sin and every evil thing
to him we turn.

2 We trust in Christ to save;
in him new life begins:
who by his cross a ransom gave
for all our sins.
Our spirits' strength and stay
who when all flesh is dust
will keep us in that final day,
in him we trust.

3 We would be true to him
till earthly journeys end,
whose love no passing years can dim,
our changeless friend.
May we who bear his Name
our faith and love renew,
to follow Christ our single aim,
and find him true.

Timothy Dudley-Smith (b. 1926)

95 *When God the Spirit came*

FIRST TUNE

MALONE 66 86 66

William Donald Davison (b. 1937)

1 When God the Spirit came
   upon his Church outpoured
   in sound of wind and sign of flame
   they spread his truth abroad,
   and filled with the Spirit
   proclaimed that Christ is Lord.

2 What courage, power and grace
   that youthful Church displayed!
   To those of every tribe and race
   they witnessed unafraid,
   and filled with the Spirit
   they broke their bread and prayed.

3 They saw God's word prevail,
   his kingdom still increase,
   no part of all his purpose fail,
   no promised blessing cease,
   and filled with the Spirit
   knew love and joy and peace.

4 Their theme was Christ alone,
   the Lord who lived and died,
   who rose to his eternal throne
   at God the Father's side,
   and filled with the Spirit
   the Church was multiplied.

5 So to this present hour
   our task is still the same,
   in pentecostal love and power
   his gospel to proclaim,
   and filled with the Spirit,
   rejoice in Jesus' name.

Timothy Dudley-Smith (b. 1926)

SECOND TUNE

LIMERICK   66 86 66

Edward Flewett Darling (b. 1933)

With vigour
Unison

1 When God the Spirit came
upon his Church outpoured
in sound of wind and sign of flame
they spread his truth abroad,
and filled with the Spirit
proclaimed that Christ is Lord.

2 What courage, power and grace
that youthful Church displayed!
To those of every tribe and race
they witnessed unafraid,
and filled with the Spirit
they broke their bread and prayed.

3 They saw God's word prevail,
his kingdom still increase,
no part of all his purpose fail,
no promised blessing cease,
and filled with the Spirit
knew love and joy and peace.

4 Their theme was Christ alone,
the Lord who lived and died,
who rose to his eternal throne
at God the Father's side,
and filled with the Spirit
the Church was multiplied.

5 So to this present hour
our task is still the same,
in pentecostal love and power
his gospel to proclaim,
and filled with the Spirit,
rejoice in Jesus' name.

Timothy Dudley-Smith (b. 1926)
based on Acts 2

96 *When Jesus came to Jordan*

CRÜGER   76 76 D

Johann Crüger (1598–1662)

For a slight variation in the harmony of this tune see *Irish Church Hymnal* No. 418.

1 When Jesus came to Jordan
   to be baptized by John,
   he did not come for pardon,
   but as his Father's Son.
   He came to share repentance
   with all who mourn their sins,
   to speak the vital sentence
   with which good news begins.

2 He came to share temptation,
   our utmost woe and loss;
   for us and our salvation
   to die upon the cross.
   So when the Dove descended
   on him, the Son of Man,
   the hidden years had ended,
   the age of grace began.

3 Come, Holy Spirit, aid us
   to keep the vows we make;
   this very day invade us,
   and every bondage break;
   come, give our lives direction,
   the gift we covet most—
   to share the resurrection
   that leads to Pentecost.

   Frederick Pratt Green (b. 1903)

97 *When I needed a neighbour*

NEIGHBOUR

Sydney Carter (b. 1915)
arr. Donald Davison

Rather slowly

And the creed and the col-our and the name won't mat-ter, were you there?
(v.6) *I'll be there.*

1 When I needed a neighbour, were you there,
  were you there?
  When I needed a neighbour, were you there?

  *And the creed and the colour and the name
  won't matter,
  were you there?*

2 I was hungry and thirsty, were you there,
  were you there?
  I was hungry and thirsty, were you there?

3 I was cold, I was naked, were you there,
  were you there?
  I was cold, I was naked, were you there?

4 When I needed a shelter, were you there,
  were you there?
  When I needed a shelter, were you there?

5 When I needed a healer, were you there,
  were you there?
  When I needed a healer, were you there?

6 Wherever you travel, I'll be there,
  I'll be there,
  Wherever you travel, I'll be there,

  *And the creed and the colour and the name
  won't matter,
  I'll be there.*

*Sydney Carter (b. 1915)
based on Matthew 25: 31–46*

98 *Who are we?*

MONKS GATE   65 65 66 65

English traditional melody
arr. Ralph Vaughan Williams (1872–1958)

1 Who are we who stand and sing?
  We are God's people.
  What this bread and wine we bring?
  Food for God's people.
  As once with twelve Christ spake,
  poured wine, and bread did break;
  he now of us will make
  a faithful people.

2 What command does Christ impart
  to us his people?
  Soul and strength and mind and heart;
  serve me, my people.
  As he in love came low,
  our world and work to know;
  to life he bids us go
  to be his people.

3 Who are we who say one creed?
  We are God's people.
  What the word we hear and read?
  Word of God's people.
  Through time, in every race,
  from earth to farthest space,
  we'll be, with Christ's good grace,
  a faithful people.

Thomas Herbert O'Driscoll (b. 1928)

99 *Won't you let me be your servant?*
(The Servant Song)

SERVANT SONG   87 87

Richard Gillard
arr. Betty Pulkingham (b. 1928)

*Guitar chords and vocal harmonies are not designed to be used together.

1 Brother, sister, let me serve you,
   let me be as Christ to you.
   Pray that I may have the grace
   to let you be my servant, too.

2 We are pilgrims on a journey,
   and companions on the road;
   we are here to help each other
   walk the mile and bear the load.

3 I will hold the Christ-light for you
   in the night-time of your fear;
   I will hold my hand out to you,
   speak the peace you long to hear.

4 I will weep when you are weeping;
   when you laugh I'll laugh with you.
   I will share your joy and sorrow
   'til we've seen this journey through.

5 When we sing to God in heaven
   we shall find such harmony,
   born of all we've known together
   of Christ's love and agony.

6 Won't you let me be your servant,
   let me be as Christ to you?
   Pray that I may have the grace
   to let you be my servant, too.

Richard Gillard

100 *Would you walk by?*

CROSS OVER THE ROAD

Pamela Verrall
Refrain adpt. Donald Davison

At a moderate pace

1. Would you walk by on the o-ther side, when some-one called for aid?__ Would you walk by on the o-ther side, and would you be a-fraid?

A shade quicker
REFRAIN *(Optional harmony)*

Cross o-ver the road, my friend,_ ask the Lord his strength to lend,__

his com-pas-sion has no end,___ cross o-ver the road.

1 Would you walk by on the other side,
  when someone called for aid?
  Would you walk by on the other side,
  and would you be afraid?

  Cross over the road, my friend,
  ask the Lord his strength to lend,
  his compassion has no end,
  cross over the road.

2 Would you walk by on the other side,
  when you saw a loved one stray?
  Would you walk by on the other side,
  or would you watch and pray?

3 Would you walk by on the other side,
  when starving children cried?
  Would you walk by on the other side,
  and would you not provide?

Pamela Verrall
based on Luke 10: 30–7

2

HYMNS FOR USE AT
THE HOLY COMMUNION

101 *Break thou the bread of life*

BREAD OF LIFE   10 10 10 10

William Fisk Sherwin (1826–88)
harm. Donald Davison

1 Break thou the bread of life,
dear Lord, to me,
as thou didst break the loaves
beside the sea;
beyond the sacred page
I seek thee, Lord,
my spirit longs for thee,
O living Word.

2 Bless thou the truth, dear Lord,
to me, to me,
as thou didst bless the bread
by Galilee;
then shall all bondage cease,
all fetters fall,
and I shall find my peace,
my all in all.

Mary Artemisia Lathbury
(1841–1913)

102 *Christians, lift your hearts*

ALLELUIA, DULCE CARMEN 87 87 87
(TANTUM ERGO)

Melody from *An Essay on the
Church Plain Chant* (1782)

For another version of this tune in A major see *Irish Church Hymnal* No. 83.
May also be sung to REGENT SQUARE or WESTMINSTER ABBEY (*Irish Church Hymnal* Nos. 69 and 193).

1 Christians, lift your hearts and voices,
   let your praises be outpoured;
   come with joy and exultation
   to the table of the Lord;
   come believing, come expectant,
   in obedience to his word.

2 See, presiding at his table,
   Jesus Christ our great high priest;
   where he summons all his people,
   none is greatest, none is least;
   graciously he bids them welcome
   to the eucharistic feast.

3 Lord, we offer in thanksgiving
   life and work for you to bless;
   yet unworthy is the offering,
   marred by pride and carelessness;
   so, Lord, pardon our transgressions,
   plant in us true holiness.

4 On the evening of his passion
   Jesus gave the wine and bread,
   so that all who love and serve him
   shall for evermore be fed.
   Taste and see the Lord is gracious,
   feed upon the living bread.

John Edward Bowers (b. 1923)

103 *He gave his life*

ST MATTHEW   DCM

Later form of a tune in
A Supplement to the New Version (1708)
probably by William Croft (1678–1727)

For another harmonization of this tune (in C major) see *Irish Church Hymnal* No. 289.
May also be sung to KINGSFOLD (No. 69).

1 He gave his life in selfless love,
   for sinners once he came;
   he had no stain of sin himself,
   but bore our guilt and shame:
   he took the cup of pain and death,
   his blood was freely shed;
   we see his body on the cross,
   we share the living bread.

2 He did not come to call the good
   but sinners to repent;
   it was the lame, the deaf, the blind
   for whom his life was spent:
   to heal the sick, to find the lost—
   it was for such he came,
   and round his table all may come
   to praise his holy name.

3 They heard him call his Father's name—
   then 'Finished!' was his cry;
   like them we have forsaken him
   and left him there to die:
   the sins that crucified him then
   are sins his blood has cured;
   the love that bound him to a cross
   our freedom has ensured.

4 His body broken once for us
   is glorious now above;
   the cup of blessing we receive,
   a sharing of his love:
   as in his presence we partake,
   his dying we proclaim
   until the hour of majesty
   when Jesus comes again.

Christopher Porteous (b. 1935)
and in this version Jubilate Hymns

104 *I am the Bread of Life*

I Am The Bread Of Life

Suzanne Toolan (b. 1927)
Verse arr. Anthony F. Carver
Refrain arr. Betty Pulkingham (b. 1928)

Rich and full

VERSES *(Unison)*

1. 'I am the Bread of Life;____ he who comes to me shall not_
(2.) bread that_ I will give____ is my flesh for the life of the
(3.) -less you__ eat____ of the flesh of the Son of__
4. 'I am the Re-sur-rec - tion, I____ am the_
(5.) Lord,__ we be - lieve____ that_ you____ are the_

hun - ger;__ he who be-lieves in me shall not thirst.
world,__ and he who eats____ of this bread,
Man,__ and_ drink____ of his blood, and
Life.__ He who be - lieves____ in me,
Christ,__ the_ Son____ of God

Suzanne Toolan (b. 1927), based on John 6

207

105 *I come with joy*

ST BOTOLPH   CM

Gordon Archbold Slater (1896–1979)

For another setting of this tune (in E♭) see *Irish Church Hymnal* No. 597.

1 I come with joy to meet my Lord,
   forgiven, loved, and free,
   in awe and wonder to recall
   his life laid down for me.

2 I come with Christians far and near
   to find, as all are fed
   the new community of love
   in Christ's communion bread.

3 As Christ breaks bread and bids us share,
   each proud division ends.
   The love that made us, makes us one,
   and strangers now are friends.

4 And thus with joy we meet our Lord.
   His presence, always near,
   is in such friendship better known,
   we see and praise him here.

5 Together met, together bound,
   we'll go our different ways,
   and as his people in the world
   we'll live and speak his praise.

Brian Arthur Wren (b. 1936)

106 *Jesus, our Master*

SLANE 10 11 11 12

Irish traditional melody
arr. Donald Davison

For another harmonization of this tune see No. 53.
For other variations of this tune (not suitable for singing to these words) see *Irish Church Hymnal* No. 322.

1 Jesus, our Master, on the night that they came
   to take you to prison, to death and to shame,
   you called to your table the friends that you knew,
   and asked them to do this in remembrance of you.

2 Still through the ages your new friends draw near,
   and know when they do so, that you will be here;
   we know you are present, though just out of view,
   to meet those who gather in remembrance of you.

3 When it is over, and all gone away,
   come back to our thoughts for the rest of the day,
   and stay with us always, who met here to do
   the thing you commanded, in remembrance of you.

Michael Edward Hewlett (b. 1916)

107 *Jesus, stand among us*

JESUS, STAND AMONG US

Graham Kendrick (b. 1950)

1. Je-sus, stand a-mong us — at the meet-ing of our lives,
be our sweet a - gree-ment at the meet - ing of our eyes;

REFRAIN

O Je - sus, we love you, so we ga - ther here,
join our hearts in u - ni-ty — and take a - way —

This hymn may be sung at services other than the Holy Communion by omitting v.3.

1 Jesus, stand among us
at the meeting of our lives,
be our sweet agreement
at the meeting of our eyes;

O Jesus, we love you,
so we gather here,
join our hearts in unity
and take away our fear.

2 So to you we're gathering
out of each and every land,
Christ the love between us
at the joining of our hands;

3 Jesus stand among us
at the breaking of the bread,
join us as one body
as we worship you, our head.

Graham Kendrick (b. 1950)
based on Matthew 18: 20

108 *Let us break bread*

LET US BREAK BREAD

American folk-melody
arr. Donald Davison

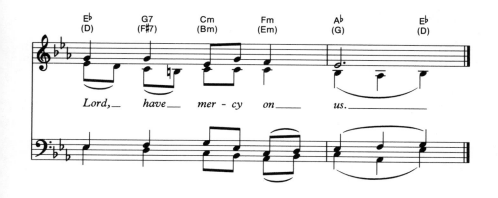

Lord,— have— mer - cy on—— us.——

1 Let us break bread together, we are one;
   let us break bread together, we are one;

   We are one as we stand*
   with our face to the risen Son,
   O Lord, have mercy on us.

2 Let us drink wine together . . . (*etc.*)

3 Let us praise God together . . . (*etc.*)

   American Traditional Folk Hymn

*The word 'kneel' may be substituted
for 'stand' when appropriate.

109 *Love is his word*

CRESSWELL   88 97 with refrain

Anthony Milner (b. 1925)

REFRAIN

Rich - er than gold   is   the
love   of   my Lord,   bet - ter than splen - dour and wealth.

1 Love is his word, love is his way,
feasting with friends, fasting alone,
living and dying, rising again,
love, only love, is his way:

Richer than gold is the love of my Lord,
better than splendour and wealth.

2 Love is his way, love is his mark,
sharing his last Passover feast.
Christ at his table, host to the twelve,
love, only love, is his mark:

3 Love is his mark, love is his sign,
bread for our strength, wine for our joy,
'This is my body, this is my blood'—
love, only love, is his sign:

4 Love is his sign, love is his news,
'Do this,' he said, 'lest you forget
all my deep sorrow, all my dear blood'—
love, only love, is his news:

5 Love is his news, love is his name,
we are his own, chosen and called,
family, brethren, cousins and kin,
love, only love, is his name:

6 Love is his name, love is his law,
hear his command, all who are his:
'Love one another, I have loved you'—
love, only love, is his law.

7 Love is his law, love is his word:
love of the Lord, Father and Word,
love of the Spirit, God ever one,
love, only love, is his word:

Luke Connaughton (1917–79)

110 *An upper room*

O WALY WALY 98 98

English traditional melody
arr. John Whitridge Wilson (b. 1905)

If any of vv.1–3 are sung by the choir alone, they may be in harmony, with A.T.B. humming
or singing a vowel sound; but v.4 should always be in unison.

The words were written for this tune.

1 An upper room did our Lord prepare
for those he loved until the end:
and his disciples still gather there,
to celebrate their risen friend.

2 A lasting gift Jesus gave his own—
to share his bread, his loving cup.
Whatever burdens may bow us down,
he by his cross shall lift us up.

3 And after supper he washed their feet,
for service, too, is sacrament.
In him our joy shall be made complete—
sent out to serve, as he was sent.

(*Organ introduction*)

4 No end there is: we depart in peace.
He loves beyond our uttermost:
in every room in our Father's house
he will be there, as Lord and host.

Frederick Pratt Green (b. 1903)

111 *At the supper*

Liebster Jesu   78 78 88

Melody by Johann Rudolph Ahle (1625–73)
harm. Johann Sebastian Bach (1685–1750)

Bar 8 has been simplified. For the original harmonization of this tune see *Irish Church Hymnal* No. 221.

1 At the supper, Christ the Lord
gathered friends and said the blessing;
bread was broken, wine was poured,
faith in Israel's God expressing:
signs of the forthcoming passion,
tokens of a great salvation.

2 After supper, Jesus knelt,
taking towel and bowl of water;
washing the disciples' feet,
servant now as well as master:
'You,' said he, 'have my example—
let your way of life be humble!'

3 In the fellowship of faith
Christ himself with us is present;
supper of the Lord in truth,
host and master all-sufficient!
From this table, gladly sharing,
send us, Lord, to love and caring.

David Mowbray (b. 1938)

112 *In the quiet consecration*

HALTON HOLGATE   87 87

Later form of tune by
William Boyce (1710–79)

May also be sung to LOVE DIVINE (*Irish Church Hymnal* No. 590).

1 In the quiet consecration
   of this glad communion hour,
   here we rest in you, Lord Jesus,
   taste your love and touch your power.

2 Here we learn through sacred symbol
   all your grace can be and do,
   by this wonderful indwelling—
   you in us, and we in you.

3 Christ the living bread from heaven,
   Christ whose blood is drink indeed,
   here by faith and with thanksgiving
   in our hearts on you we feed.

4 By your death for sin atoning,
   by your resurrection-life,
   hold us fast in joyful union,
   strengthen us to face the strife.

5 While afar in solemn radiance
   shines the feast that is to come—
   after conflict, heaven's glory,
   your great feast of love and home.

Constance Coote (1844–1936)

113 *Lord Jesus Christ*
(Living Lord)

LIVING LORD

Words and music by
Patrick Robert Norman Appleford (b. 1925)

1. Lord Je-sus Christ,_____ you_____ have come to us,
2. Lord Je-sus Christ,_____ now_____ and ev-ery day
3. Lord Je-sus Christ,_____ you_____ have come to us,
4. Lord Je-sus Christ,_____ we_____ would come to you,

you_____ are one with us, Ma - ry's son —
teach_____ us how to pray, Son of God.
born_____ as one of us, Ma - ry's son —
live_____ our lives for you, Son of God;

The unison version accompaniment is appropriate for the piano. Organists may prefer to play
the harmony version.

clean - sing   our   souls   from   all   their   sin,
You   have com - mand - ed   us   to   do
led   out   to   die   on   Cal -   va -   ry,
all   your   com - mands   we   know   are   true;

pour - ing   your   love   and   good - ness   in;
this,   in   re - mem - brance, Lord,   of   you;
ri -   sen   from death   to   set   us   free;
your   ma - ny   gifts   will   make   us   new;

Je - sus, our love for you we sing,
in - to our lives your power breaks through,
liv - ing Lord Je - sus, help us see
in - to our lives your power breaks through,

liv - ing Lord.
liv - ing Lord.
you are Lord.
liv - ing Lord.

225

114 *Put peace into each other's hands*

FIRST TUNE

ELMWOOD 87 87

Anthony Frederick Carver (b. 1947)

Smoothly, not too slow

1 Put peace into each other's hands
and like a treasure hold it,
protect it like a candle-flame,
with tenderness enfold it.

2 Put peace into each other's hands
with loving expectation;
be gentle in your words and ways
in touch with God's creation.

3 Put peace into each other's hands,
like bread we break for sharing;
look people warmly in the eye:
our life is meant for caring.

4 As at communion, shape your hands
into a waiting cradle;
the gift of Christ receive, revere,
united round the table.

5 Put Christ into each other's hands,
he is love's deepest measure;
in love make peace, give peace a chance
and share it like a treasure.

Frederik Herman Kaan (b. 1929)

SECOND TUNE

William Donald Davison (b. 1937)

Tenderly, with gentle movement

DESCANT *(v.5 – optional)*

5. Put Christ in - to each o-ther's hands,__ he is love's deep - est mea - sure; in love make peace, give peace a chance and share it like a trea - sure.

May also be sung to St Columba (*Irish Church Hymnal* No. 315), noting the alternative endings to the second and fourth lines of each verse, or to Ach Gott Und Herr (*Irish Church Hymnal* No. 243).

115   *We come as guests invited*

KINGS LYNN   76 76 D

English traditional melody
arr. Ralph Vaughan Williams (1872–1958)

Dignified
Unison

May also be sung to AURELIA (*Irish Church Hymnal* No. 430).

1 We come as guests invited
when Jesus bids us dine,
his friends on earth united
to share the bread and wine;
the bread of life is broken,
the wine is freely poured,
for us, in solemn token
of Christ our dying Lord.

2 We eat and drink, receiving
from Christ the grace we need,
and in our hearts believing
on him by faith we feed;
with wonder and thanksgiving
for love that knows no end,
we find in Jesus living
our ever-present friend.

3 One bread is ours for sharing,
one single fruitful vine,
our fellowship declaring
renewed in bread and wine—
renewed, sustained and given
by token, sign and word,
the pledge and seal of heaven,
the love of Christ our Lord.

Timothy Dudley-Smith (b. 1926)

116 *You satisfy the hungry heart*
(Gift of finest wheat)

GIFT OF FINEST WHEAT   Robert E. Kreutz

With simple lyricism
Unison

You sa - tis - fy the hun-gry heart___ with

gift of fin - est wheat; come, give to us, O___

sav-ing Lord, the bread of life to eat.___

1. As when the shep - herd calls his sheep, they

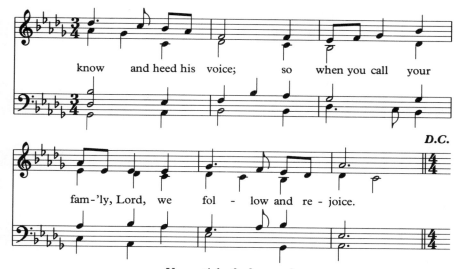

know and heed his voice; so when you call your

D.C.

fam-'ly, Lord, we fol - low and re - joice.

You satisfy the hungry heart
with gift of finest wheat;
come, give to us, O saving Lord,
the bread of life to eat.

1 As when the shepherd calls his sheep,
they know and heed his voice;
so when you call your fam'ly, Lord,
we follow and rejoice.

2 With joyful lips we sing to you
our praise and gratitude,
that you should count us worthy, Lord,
to share this heav'nly food.

3 Is not the cup we bless and share
the blood of Christ outpoured?
Do not one cup, one loaf declare
our oneness in the Lord?

4 The myst'ry of your presence, Lord,
no mortal tongue can tell:
whom all the world cannot contain
comes in our hearts to dwell.

5 You give yourself to us, O Lord;
then selfless let us be,
to serve each other in your name
in truth and charity.

Omer Westendorf (b. 1916)

231

117 *Alleluia! Alleluia! Opening our hearts*
(Jesus is our King!)

POST GREEN

Sherrell Prebble

Al - le-lu - ia! Al - le - lu - ia! O - pen - ing our
hearts to him, sing - ing al - le - lu - ia!
Al - le - lu - ia! Je - sus is our King!

VERSES *(Optional harmony)* *

Sherrell Prebble and Howard Clark

*Guitar chords should not be used in the verses if these are sung in harmony.

233

118 *As we walk along beside you*

BURNING HEART   Norman Leonard Warren (b. 1934)

Al - le - lu - ia, al - le - lu - - ia!

Lord, al - le - lu - ia!

Alleluia, alleluia!

1 As we walk along beside you,
  and we hear you speak of mercy,
  then it seems our hearts are burning
  for we find you in the sharing of the word.

2 As we ask that you stay with us
  and we watch what you are doing,
  then our eyes begin to open
  for we see you in the breaking of the bread.

3 As we reach for you believing
  and we go to love and serve you,
  then our lives will be proclaiming
  that we know you in the rising from the dead.

  Lord, alleluia!

Michael Arnold Perry (b. 1942)
based on Luke 24: 13–35

119 *Father, who in Jesus found us*

QUEM PASTORES   88 87

15th-century German carol melody
arr. Ralph Vaughan Williams (1872–1958)

1 Father, who in Jesus found us,
  God, whose love is all around us,
  who to freedom new unbound us,
  keep our hearts with joy aflame.

2 For the sacramental breaking,
  for the honour of partaking,
  for your life our lives remaking,
  young and old, we praise your name.

3 From the service of this table
  lead us to a life more stable;
  for our witness make us able;
  blessing on our work we claim.

4 Through our calling closely knitted,
  daily to your praise committed,
  for a life of service fitted,
  let us now your love proclaim.

Frederik Herman Kaan (b. 1929)

120 *For the bread which you have broken*

Sʜɪᴘsᴛᴏɴ   87 87

English traditional melody
arr. Ralph Vaughan Williams (1872–1958)

For a slightly different harmonization of this tune see *Irish Church Hymnal* No. 301.
May also be sung to Hᴀʟᴛᴏɴ Hᴏʟɢᴀᴛᴇ (No. 112) or Sᴛ Nɪᴄʜᴏʟᴀs (*Irish Church Hymnal* No. 166).

1 For the bread which you have broken,
for the wine which you have poured,
for the words which you have spoken,
now we give you thanks, O Lord.

2 By these pledges that you love us,
by your gift of peace restored,
by your call to heaven above us,
hallow all our lives, O Lord.

3 In your service, Lord, defend us,
in our hearts keep watch and ward;
in the world to which you send us
let your kingdom come, O Lord.

Louis Fitzgerald Benson (1855–1930)

121 *Now let us from this table rise*

NIAGARA LM

Robert Jackson (1840–1914)

May also be sung to SOLOTHURN (*Irish Church Hymnal* No. 183).

1 Now let us from this table rise
renewed in body, mind and soul;
with Christ we die and live again,
his selfless love has made us whole.

2 With minds alert, upheld by grace,
to spread the Word in speech and deed,
we follow in the steps of Christ,
at one with all in hope and need.

3 To fill each human house with love,
it is the sacrament of care;
the work that Christ began to do
we humbly pledge ourselves to share.

4 Then give us courage, Father God,
to choose again the pilgrim way,
and help us to accept with joy
the challenge of tomorrow's day.

Frederik Herman Kaan (b. 1929)

122 *One bread, one body*

ONE BREAD, ONE BODY

Words and music by John B. Foley

ma-ny,_____ through-out the earth,_____ we are one

Last time
to Coda ⊕ **a tempo**
rit.

bo - dy in this one_____ Lord.

Slightly faster, with excitement

VERSES
f marcato

1. Gen-tile or Jew, ser-vant or
2. Ma-ny the gifts, ma-ny the
3. Grain for the fields, scat-tered and

f Sw.

free,   wo - man or man,_____
works,   one in the Lord_____
grown,   ga-thered to one,_____

rit.

D.S.
(p.239)

no more._____
of all._____
for all._____

One

CODA

a tempo   rit.

*Lord.*_____

based on 1 Corinthians 10: 16–17, 12: 4;
Galatians 3: 28; The Didache, 9

241

123 *Praise the Lord*

EVANGELISTS   887 D
(ALLES IST AN GOTTES SEGEN)

Adapted from J. S. Bach's
version of a chorale
by J. Löhner (1691) and others

For another setting of this tune (in G major) see *Irish Church Hymnal* No. 200.

1 Praise the Lord, rise up rejoicing,
worship, thanks, devotion voicing:
glory be to God on high!
Christ, your cross and passion sharing,
by this Eucharist declaring
yours the eternal victory.

2 Scattered flock, one Shepherd sharing,
lost and lonely, one voice hearing,
ears are open to your word;
by your blood new life receiving,
in your body firm, believing,
we are yours, and you the Lord.

3 Send us forth alert and living,
sins forgiven, wrongs forgiving,
in your Spirit strong and free.
Finding love in all creation,
bringing peace in every nation,
may we faithful followers be.

Howard Charles Adie Gaunt (1902–83)

124 *Sent forth by God's blessing*

THE ASH GROVE   12 11 12 11 D

Welsh traditional melody
arr. Gerald Hocker Knight (1908–79)

1 Sent forth by God's blessing, our true faith confessing,
   the people of God from his dwelling take leave.
   The supper is ended; O now be extended
   the fruits of his service in all who believe.
   The seed of his teaching, our hungry souls reaching,
   shall blossom in action for God and for all.
   His grace shall incite us, his love shall unite us
   to further God's kingdom and answer his call.

2 With praise and thanksgiving to God who is living,
   the tasks of our everyday life we will face.
   Our faith ever sharing, in love ever caring,
   we claim as our neighbour all those of each race.
   One bread that has fed us, one light that has led us
   unite us as one in his life that we share.
   Then may all the living with praise and thanksgiving
   give honour to Christ and his name that we bear.

Omer Westendorf (b. 1916), altd.

125 *The Lord is here*

WOODLANDS 10 10 10 10

Walter Greatorex (1877–1949)

1. The Lord is here – he finds us as we seek to learn his will and fol - low in his way. He gives him - self just

The accompaniment is given here in its original form. For a simpler version see No. 136.

as he gave his Word, the God of
pro - mise greets us ev - 'ry day.

1 The Lord is here—he finds us as we seek
   to learn his will and follow in his way.
   He gives himself just as he gave his Word,
   the God of promise greets us ev'ry day.

2 The Lord is here—he meets us as we share—
   this is the life he calls us now to live;
   in offered peace, in shared-out bread and wine,
   our God is gift and calls us now to give.

3 The Lord is here—inviting us to go
   and share the news with people everywhere.
   He waits outside in need and help alike,
   the Spirit moves through deed as well as prayer.

4 So let us go, intent to seek and find,
   living this hope that God is always near.
   Sharing and trusting, let us live his love,
   that all the world may say—'The Lord is here.'

Christopher Ellis (b. 1949)

3

HYMNS BASED ON
THE CANTICLES

126 *All created things*
(Benedicite)

FIRST SETTING

Kᴜᴍ Bᴀ Yᴀʜ   77 77

West Indian traditional melody
arr. Donald Davison

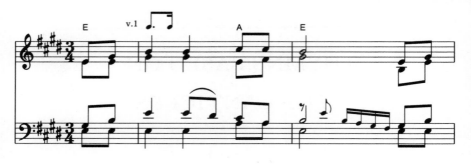

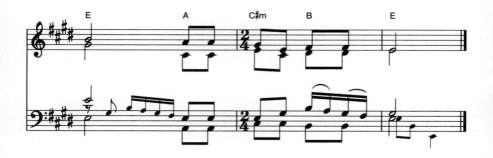

1 All created things, bless the Lord;
   all you heavens, bless the Lord;
   all you angels, bless the Lord;
   sing to God and praise his name.

2 Sun and moon and stars of heaven,
   rain and dew and winds that blow,
   fire and heat and ice and snow,
   sing to God and praise his name.

3 Bless the Lord, you nights and days;
   light and darkness, praise him too;
   clouds and lightnings in the sky,
   sing to God and praise his name.

4 Hills and mountains, bless the Lord;
   flowing rivers with the seas,
   flying birds and earthly beasts,
   sing to God and praise his name.

5 All who dwell upon the earth,
   priests and servants of the Lord,
   humble people, holy ones,
   sing to God and praise his name.

6 Bless the Father, bless the Son,
   bless the Spirit, Three in One;
   sound his glory all your days;
   give to God exalted praise.

Edward Flewett Darling (b. 1933)

SECOND SETTING

KUM BA YAH   77 77

West Indian traditional melody
arr. Donald Davison

1. All cre - at - ed things, bless the Lord; all you hea - vens, bless the Lord; all you an - gels, bless the Lord; sing to God and praise his name.

If preferred, the accompaniment to v.1 may be used for some or all of the other verses.

252

2. Sun and moon and stars of heaven, rain and

dew and winds that blow, fire and heat and ice and

snow, sing to God and praise his name.

3. Bless the Lord, you nights and days; light and dark-ness, praise him too; clouds and light - nings in the sky, sing to God and praise his name.

254

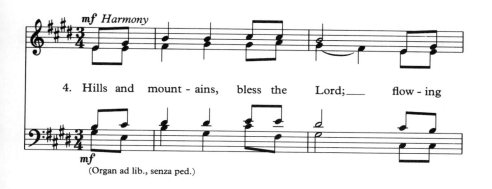

4. Hills and mount - ains, bless the Lord;___ flow - ing

(Organ ad lib., senza ped.)

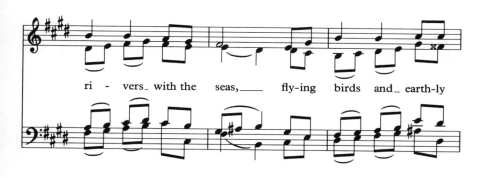

ri - vers_ with the seas,___ fly-ing birds and_ earth-ly

beasts,___ sing to God and praise his name.___

TENORS AND BASSES
(OR SOPRANOS AND ALTOS)

5. All who dwell up - on the earth, priests and ser - vants of the Lord, hum-ble peo - ple, ho - ly ones, sing to God and praise his name.

mf Gt. or Ch. 8'

Man.

Edward Flewett Darling (b. 1933)

257

127 *Bless the Lord*

BLESS THE LORD

William Donald Davison (b. 1937)

Steadily, at a moderate pace

INTRODUCTION

Unison
(Solo, Semi-chorus, or All)

1. Bless the Lord, the God of our fa - thers:*
2. Bless his ho - ly and glo - rious name:___
3. Bless him in his ho - ly and glo - rious tem - ple:

(All)

Sing his praise and ex - alt ___ him for ev - er.

*The word 'forebears' may be substituted for 'fathers' if desired.
Where the melody is adapted to fit the words, the accompaniment should be altered accordingly.

from the *Alternative Prayer Book (1984)*

128 *Blest be the God of Israel*
(Benedictus)

FIRST TUNE

CLAUDIUS DCM

Adapted from a song by G. W. Fink (1783–1846)
arr. Sydney Hugo Nicholson (1875–1947)

1 Blest be the God of Israël,
   the everlasting Lord.
   You come in power to save your own,
   your people Israël.
   For Israël you now raise up
   salvation's tower on high
   in David's house who reigned as king
   and servant of the Lord.

2 Through holy prophets did you speak
   your word in days of old,
   that you would save us from our foes
   and all who bear us ill.
   On Sinaï you gave to us
   your covenant of love;
   so with us now you keep your word
   in love that knows no end.

3 Of old you gave your solemn oath
   to Father Abraham;
   whose seed a mighty race should be
   and blest for evermore.
   You vowed to set your people free
   from fear of every foe,
   that we might serve you all our days
   in goodness, love, and peace.

4 O tiny child, your name shall be
   the prophet of the Lord;
   the way of God you will prepare
   to make God's coming known.
   You shall proclaim to Israël
   salvation's dawning day,
   when God shall wipe away all sins
   with mercy and with love.

5 The rising sun shall shine on us
   to bring the light of day
   to all who sit in darkest night
   and shadow of the grave.
   Our footsteps God shall safely guide
   to walk the ways of peace,
   whose name for evermore be blest,
   who lives and loves and saves.

James Quinn (b. 1919), altd. 1985
based on Luke 1: 68–79

Words © 1969, 1985 James Quinn SJ. Reprinted by permission of Geoffrey Chapman, an imprint of Cassell Publishers Ltd.,
Artillery House, Artillery Row, London SW1P 1RT.

SECOND TUNE

St Asaph DCM

Smith's *Sacred Music*, Edinburgh (1825)
possibly by Giovanni Marie Giornovichi (1745–1804)

May also be sung to Kingsfold (No. 69) or Forest Green (*Irish Church Hymnal* No. 66).

1 Blest be the God of Israël,
  the everlasting Lord.
  You come in power to save your own,
  your people Israël.
  For Israël you now raise up
  salvation's tower on high
  in David's house who reigned as king
  and servant of the Lord.

2 Through holy prophets did you speak
  your word in days of old,
  that you would save us from our foes
  and all who bear us ill.
  On Sinaï you gave to us
  your covenant of love;
  so with us now you keep your word
  in love that knows no end.

3 Of old you gave your solemn oath
  to Father Abraham;
  whose seed a mighty race should be
  and blest for evermore.
  You vowed to set your people free
  from fear of every foe,
  that we might serve you all our days
  in goodness, love, and peace.

4 O tiny child, your name shall be
  the prophet of the Lord;
  the way of God you will prepare
  to make God's coming known.
  You shall proclaim to Israël
  salvation's dawning day,
  when God shall wipe away all sins
  with mercy and with love.

5 The rising sun shall shine on us
  to bring the light of day
  to all who sit in darkest night
  and shadow of the grave.
  Our footsteps God shall safely guide
  to walk the ways of peace,
  whose name for evermore be blest,
  who lives and loves and saves.

James Quinn (b. 1919), altd. 1985
based on Luke 1: 68–79

129 Come, worship God
(Venite)

VENITE 11 10 11 10

William Donald Davison (b. 1937)

Light and rhythmic, but not too fast

1. Come, wor-ship God who is wor-thy of hon-our, en-ter his pre-sence with thanks and a song! He is the rock of his peo-ple's sal-va-tion, to whom our ju-bi-lant prais-es be-long.

May also be sung to O QUANTA QUALIA (No. 38) or to the setting of the same tune in the *Irish Church Hymnal* (No. 441).

⊕ *CODA* **molto rall.**

trust in his pro - mis - es, walk in his ways!

1 Come, worship God who is worthy of honour,
   enter his presence with thanks and a song!
   He is the rock of his people's salvation,
   to whom our jubilant praises belong.

2 Ruled by his might are the heights of the mountains,
   held in his hands are the depths of the earth;
   his is the sea, his the land, for he made them,
   king above all gods, who gave us our birth.

3 We are his people, the sheep of his pasture,
   he is our maker and to him we pray;
   gladly we kneel in obedience before him—
   great is the God whom we worship this day!

4 Now let us listen, for God speaks among us,
   open our hearts and receive what he says:
   peace be to all who remember his goodness,
   trust in his promises, walk in his ways!

Michael Arnold Perry (b. 1942)
based on Psalm 95: 1–7

130 *Faithful vigil ended*
(Nunc dimittis)

PASTOR PASTORUM   65 65   Friedrich Philipp Silcher (1789–1860)

May also be sung to GLENFINLAS (No. 17).

1 Faithful vigil ended,
watching, waiting cease:
Master, grant your servant
his discharge in peace.

2 All your Spirit promised,
all the Father willed,
now these eyes behold it
perfectly fulfilled.

3 This your great deliverance
sets your people free;
Christ their light uplifted
all the nations see.

4 Christ, your people's glory!
Watching, doubting cease:
grant to us your servants
our discharge in peace.

Timothy Dudley-Smith (b. 1926)
based on Luke 2: 29–32

131 *Glory and honour and power*

GLORY AND HONOUR

William Donald Davison (b. 1937)

Steadily, at a moderate pace

1. Glo-ry and hon-our and power: are yours by right, O Lord our God. 2. For you cre-a-ted all things: and by your will they have their be-ing. 3. Glo-ry and hon-our and

power: are yours by right, O Lamb for us slain;— 4. for by your

blood you ran-somed men* for God: from

ev - 'ry race and lan-guage, from ev - 'ry peo - ple and

na - tion, 5. to make them* a king - dom of

*The word 'us' may be substituted for 'men' and 'them' where indicated, if desired.

priests: to stand and serve be -

- fore our_ God.___ 6. To him who sits on the throne and to the

Lamb: be praise and hon - our,

rall. *Optional descant*

glo - ry and might for ev - er and ev - er. A - men.

from the Alternative Prayer Book (1984)

132 *Glory in the highest*
(Gloria in excelsis)

Cuddesdon   65 65 D

William Harold Ferguson (1874–1950)

May also be sung to Camberwell (No. 143) or Evelyns (*Irish Church Hymnal* No. 373).

1 Glory in the highest to the God of heaven!
  Peace to all your people through the earth be given:
  mighty God and Father, thanks and praise we bring,
  singing alleluias to our heavenly King.

2 Jesus Christ is risen, God the Father's Son:
  with the Holy Spirit, you are Lord alone!
  Lamb once killed for sinners, all our guilt to bear,
  show us now your mercy, now receive our prayer.

3 Christ the world's true Saviour, high and holy one,
  seated now and reigning from your Father's throne:
  Lord and God, we praise you; highest heaven adores:
  in the Father's glory, all the praise be yours!

Christopher Martin Idle (b. 1938)

133 *God, we praise you*
(Te Deum)

RUSTINGTON   87 87 D

Charles Hubert Hastings Parry
(1848–1918)

May also be sung to ABBOT'S LEIGH (No. 16), BLAENWERN (No. 30), or HYFRYDOL
(*Irish Church Hymnal* No. 43).

1 God, we praise you! God, we bless you!
God, we name you sovereign Lord!
Mighty King whom angels worship,
Father, by your Church adored:
all creation shows your glory,
heaven and earth draw near your throne,
singing, 'Holy, holy, holy,
Lord of hosts, and God alone!'

2 True apostles, faithful prophets,
saints who set their world ablaze,
martyrs, once unknown, unheeded,
join one growing song of praise,
while your Church on earth confesses
one majestic Trinity:
Father, Son, and Holy Spirit,
God, our hope eternally.

3 Jesus Christ, the King of glory,
everlasting Son of God,
humble was your virgin mother,
hard the lonely path you trod:
by your cross is sin defeated,
hell confronted face to face,
heaven opened to believers,
sinners justified by grace.

4 Christ, at God's right hand victorious,
you will judge the world you made:
Lord, in mercy help your servants
for whose freedom you have paid:
raise us up from dust to glory,
guard us from all sin today;
King enthroned above all praises,
save your people, God, we pray.

Christopher Martin Idle (b. 1938)

134 *Holy, holy, holy Lord*
(Sanctus)

SANCTUS

Franz Peter Schubert (1797–1828)
(from *Deutsche Messe*, 1826)
Descant by Donald Davison

Ho - ly, ho - ly, ho - ly Lord, God of power and might,___ Ho - ly, ho - ly, ho - ly Lord, God of power and might,___ heav'n and earth are full,___ full___ of your glo - ry.

135 *Jubilate everybody*
(Jubilate Deo)

PSALM 100

Fred Dunn

With vigour
Unison

Ju - bi-la - te, ev-'ry-bo-dy, serve the Lord in all your ways, and come be-fore his pre - sence sing-ing: en - ter now his_ courts with praise. For the Lord our God is gra-cious, and his mer - cy ev - er - last - ing.

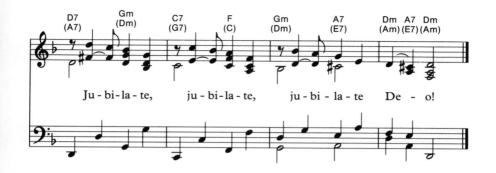

Ju - bi-la - te,   ju - bi-la - te,   ju - bi - la - te   De - o!

Jubilate, ev'rybody,
serve the Lord in all your ways,
and come before his presence singing:
enter now his courts with praise.
For the Lord our God is gracious,
and his mercy everlasting.
Jubilate, jubilate, jubilate Deo!

from Psalm 100, para. Fred Dunn

136 *Tell out, my soul*
(Magnificat)

WOODLANDS   10 10 10 10

Walter Greatorex (1877–1949)

For the original version of the accompaniment see No. 125.

1 Tell out, my soul, the greatness of the Lord:
   unnumbered blessings, give my spirit voice;
   tender to me the promise of his word;
   in God my Saviour shall my heart rejoice.

2 Tell out, my soul, the greatness of his name:
   make known his might, the deeds his arm has done;
   his mercy sure, from age to age the same;
   his holy name, the Lord, the Mighty One.

3 Tell out, my soul, the greatness of his might:
   powers and dominions lay their glory by;
   proud hearts and stubborn wills are put to flight,
   the hungry fed, the humble lifted high.

4 Tell out, my soul, the glories of his word:
   firm is his promise, and his mercy sure.
   Tell out, my soul, the greatness of the Lord
   to children's children and for evermore.

Timothy Dudley-Smith (b. 1926)
based on Luke 1: 46–55

137 *Living Lord, our praise we render!*
(Easter Anthems)

K<small>ILLALOE</small>   87 87   Edward Flewett Darling (b. 1933)

May also be sung to S<small>T</small> A<small>MBROSE</small> (S<small>T</small> O<small>SWALD</small>) (*Irish Church Hymnal* No. 180).

1 Living Lord, our praise we render!
His the blood for sinners shed.
In the Father's power and splendour
Christ is risen from the dead.

2 Death's dominion burst and broken
by that Life which no more dies;
we to whom the Lord has spoken,
one with Christ, in freedom rise.

3 One with Christ, both dead and risen;
dead to self and Satan's claim,
raised from death and sin's dark prison,
life is ours through Jesus' name.

Timothy Dudley-Smith (b. 1926)
based on Romans 6: 5–11

4

IRISH HYMNS

with English Singing Translations

138 *Dia do bheath' a naoidhe naoimh*
(All hail and welcome, holy child)

LUINNEACH

Irish traditional melody
arr. Peter Downey (b. 1956)

1. Di - a do bheath' a naoi - dhe naoimh, 'sa mhain-séar cé taoi
2. Di - a do bheath' a Íos - a 'rís! 'Do bhea-tha, i gclí on
3. Mí - le fáil - te 'nocht i gclí le mo chroí - se dom Rí

bocht_____ meadh - rach_____ sai - bhir
Ó - igh! A Ghnu - ís is
fial,_____ i ndá_____ ná - dur 'do

a tá tú 's glór-mhar id dhún féin a - nocht._____
áille ná'n ghrian, na míl - te fáil - te_____ 'do Dhi - a óg!
chu - aigh, póg is fáil - te u - aim do Dhi - a!

Irish Church Hymnal No. 621 (HIBERNIA) is a variant of this tune, but is not suitable for singing to this Christmas carol.

1. *All hail and wel - come, ho - ly child, you poor babe in the*
2. *God bless you, Je - sus, once a-gain! Your life in its young*
3. *To-night we greet you in the flesh; my heart a-dores my*

man - ger. So hap - py and rich it
bo - dy, your face____ more love - ly
young____ King. You came____ to us in

is you are to - night___ in - side___ your cas - tle.
than the sun — a thou - sand wel - comes, Ba - by!
hu - man form — I bring you a kiss and a greet - ing.

1 Dia do bheath' a naoidhe naoimh,
 'sa mhainséar cé taoi bocht
 meadhrach saibhir a tá tú
 's glórmhar id dhún féin anocht.

2 Dia do bheath' a Íosa 'rís!
 'Do bheatha, i gclí on Óigh!
 A Ghnuís is áille ná'n ghrian,
 na mílte fáilte 'do Dhia óg!

3 Míle fáilte 'nocht i gclí
 le mo chroíse dom Rí fial,
 i ndá nádur 'do chuaigh, póg
 is fáilte uaim do Dhia!

Aodh Mac Cathmhaoil
(1571–1626)
adpt. Peter Downey (b. 1956)

1 *All hail and welcome, holy child,*
 you poor babe in the manger.
 So happy and rich it is you are
 tonight inside your castle.

2 *God bless you, Jesus, once again!*
 Your life in its young body,
 your face more lovely than the sun—
 a thousand welcomes, Baby!

3 *Tonight we greet you in the flesh;*
 my heart adores my young King.
 You came to us in human form—
 I bring you a kiss and a greeting.

tr. George Otto Simms
(b. 1910)

283

139 *Ag Críost an síol*
(The seed is Christ's)

AG CRÍOST AN SÍOL

Séan Ó Riada (1931–71)
adpt. Anthony F. Carver

1. Ag__ Críost an síol; ag__ Críost an__ fómhar. In
1. The__ seed is Christ's, and__ his the__ sheaf; with -

ioth - (a) - lainn Dé go__ dtug - tar sinn. 2. Ag__
- in__ God's barn may__ we__ be stored. 2. The__

Críost an mhuir; ag__ Críost an__ t-iasc. I__
sea is Christ's; and__ his the__ fish; in the

líon - ta Dé go___ gcas - tar sinn. 3. Ó___
nets___ of God may___ we___ be caught. *3. From*

fhás go___ haois, is ó aois go____ bás, do___
birth to___ youth, and from youth till____ death, your__

dhá láimh, a Críost, a - nall thar - ainn. 4. Ó___
two hands, O Christ, stretch o - ver____ us. *4. From*

bhás go críoch, ní___ críoch ach ath-fhás, i___
death – the end? No___ end – but new life in___

bPar-thas na nGrást go___ rabh - ai-mid.
sweet Pa - ra - dise may___ we be found.

1 Ag Críost an síol;
  ag Críost an fómhar.
  In iothlainn Dé
  go dtugtar sinn.

1 *The seed is Christ's,*
  and his the sheaf;
  within God's barn
  may we be stored.

2 Ag Críost an mhuir;
  ag Críost an t-iasc.
  I líonta Dé
  go gcastar sinn.

2 *The sea is Christ's;*
  and his the fish;
  in the nets of God
  may we be caught.

3 Ó fhás go haois,
  is ó aois go bás,
  do dhá láimh, a Críost,
  anall tharainn.

3 *From birth to youth,*
  and from youth till death,
  your two hands, O Christ,
  stretch over us.

4 Ó bhás go críoch,
  ní críoch ach athfhás,
  i bParthas na nGrást
  go rabhaimid.

4 *From death—the end?*
  No end—but new life
  in sweet Paradise
  may we be found.

Anon.

tr. George Otto Simms
(b. 1910)

286

140 *Álainn farraige spéirghlas*
(Beautiful the green-blue sea)

LOVELY THE WORLD

Scots Gaelic traditional melody
arr. Donald Davison

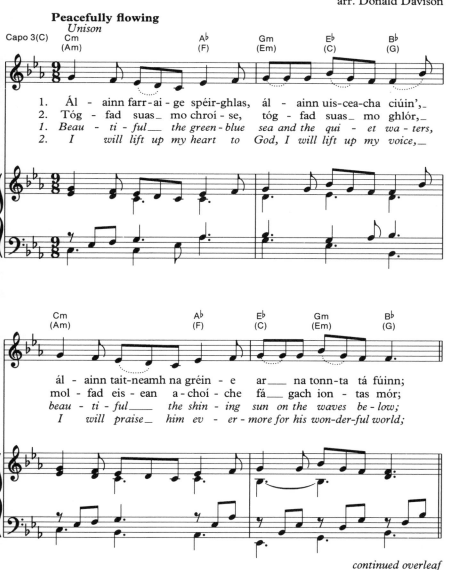

Peacefully flowing
Unison

Capo 3(C)

1. Ál - ainn farr-ai-ge spéir-ghlas, ál - ainn uis-cea-cha ciúin',_
2. Tóg - fad suas_ mo chroí - se, tóg - fad suas_ mo ghlór,_
1. *Beau - ti - ful__ the green-blue sea and the qui - et wa-ters,*
2. *I will lift up my heart to God, I will lift up my voice,_*

ál - ainn tait-neamh na gréin - e ar__ na tonn-ta tá fúinn;
mol - fad eis - ean a-choí - che fá__ gach ion - tas mór;
beau - ti - ful__ the shin - ing sun on the waves be - low;
I will praise_ him ev - er - more for his won-der-ful world;

continued overleaf

faoil - eáin 'g eit-eal 'sna spéar - tha, teas le héi - rí an lae;
ar - daigh feas-ta mo smaoin - te mar na sléibh-te san aer,
sea - gulls fly - ing a - bove as warmth re - turns with the day;
like the wa - ter clear my heart will now__ be calm,

Ó! nach ál-ainn an saol!___ Ó! nach ál-ainn, a Dhé!
ciún-aigh feas-ta mo chroí - se mar an t-uisc-e soil-éir;
O how love-ly the world is! O, how love-ly, O God!
like the hills in the air my thoughts will now__ a - rise,

Siúd uait amh - arc na sléibh - te barr' á bhfol-ach fá cheo,___
éist lem ach(ai)-ní, a Thiar - na, tar is có-naigh im chléibh,
See the hills__ be-yond, their sum - mits cov-ered in mist, and
hear my prayer, O Lord, O come, with-in__ me dwell, pre -

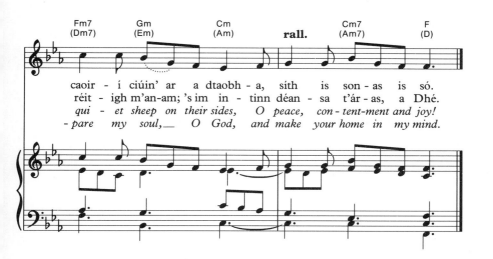

caoir - í ciúin' ar a dtaobh - a, síth is son - as is só.
réit - igh m'an-am; 's im in - tinn déan - sa t'ár - as, a Dhé.
qui - et sheep on their sides, O peace, con - tent-ment and joy!
- pare my soul,__ O God, and make your home in my mind.

1 Álainn farraige spéirghlas,
álainn uisceacha ciúin',
álainn taitneamh na gréine
ar na tonnta tá fúinn;
faoileáin 'g eiteal 'sna spéartha,
teas le héirí an lae;
Ó! nach álainn an saol!
Ó! nach álainn, a Dhé!
Siúd uait amharc na sléibhte
barr' á bhfolach fá cheo,
caoirí ciúin' ar a dtaobha,
síth is sonas is só.

2 Tógfad suas mo chroíse,
tógfad suas mo ghlór,
molfad eisean achoíche
fá gach iontas mór;
ardaigh feasta mo smaointe
mar na sléibhte san aer,
ciúnaigh feasta mo chroíse
mar an t-uisce soiléir;
éist lem achainí, a Thiarna,
tar is cónaigh im chléibh,
réitigh m'anam; 's im intinn
déansa t'áras, a Dhé.

1 *Beautiful the green-blue sea*
and the quiet waters,
beautiful the shining sun
on the waves below;
seagulls flying above
as warmth returns with the day;
O, how lovely the world is!
O, how lovely, O God!
See the hills beyond,
their summits covered in mist,
and quiet sheep on their sides,
O peace, contentment and joy!

2 *I will lift up my heart to God,*
I will lift up my voice,
I will praise him evermore
for his wonderful world;
***like the water clear*
my heart will now be calm,
like the hills in the air
my thoughts will now arise,
hear my prayer, O Lord,
O come, within me dwell,
prepare my soul, O God,
and make your home in my mind.

Douglas Hyde (An Craoibhin)
(1860–1949)

tr. Anon.
adpt. Donald Davison

*At this point the line order differs
from that in the original.

141 Bí, a Íosa, im chroíse
(O Jesus, every moment)

Bí, A Íosa

Irish traditional melody
arr. Anthony F. Carver

Unison

1. Bí, a Ío - sa, im__ chroí - se i__ gcuimh-ne gach__
2. 'Sé__ Ío - sa mo__ rí - se, mo__ cha - ra is__ mo
3. Bí, a Ío - sa, go__ síor - aí im__ chroí is im__

uair, bí, a Ío - sa, im__ chroí - se le__
ghrá; 'sé__ Ío - sa mo__ dhíd - ean ar__
bhéal, bí, a Ío - sa, go__ síor - aí im__

haith - rí__ go__ luath, bí, a Ío - sa,__ im__
pheac - aí__ is ar bhás; 'sé__ Ío - sa__ mo__
thuig - se__ mar an gcéann', bí, a Ío - sa,__ go__

May be sung unaccompanied.

290

chroí - se le___ cum - ann___ go___ buan, ó, a
aoibh - neas, mo___ scá - thán___ de___ ghnáth; is a
síor - aí im___ mheabh - air___ mar___ léann, 's ó, a

Ío - sa, 'Dhé dhí - lis, ná___ scar thu - sa uaim.
Ío - sa, 'Dhé dhí - lis, ná___ scar uaim go brách.
Ío - sa, 'Dhé dhí - lis, ná___ fág mé liom féin.

1. O___ Je - sus, ev - 'ry mo - ment be___ in my heart and
2. O___ Je - sus is my king,___ my___ friend, and my___
3. O___ Je - sus, be for ev - er in my heart and my___

mind; O___ Je - sus, stir___ my___ heart with sor - row___ for my
love; O___ Je - sus is my shel - ter from sin - ning___ and from
mouth; O___ Je - sus, be for ev - er in my thought and___ my___

sins; O Je - sus,___ fill___ my___ heart with___ ne - ver - fail-ing
death; O Je - sus,___ my___ glad - ness, my___ mir - ror___ all my
prayer; O Je - sus,___ be for ev - er in___ my qui - et___

291

love; O— Je-sus, sweet Mas-ter, ne-ver part_ from me.
days; O— Je-sus, my_ dear-est Lord, ne-ver part_ from me.
mind; O— Je-sus, my_ sweet Lord, do_ not leave me a-lone.

1 Bí, a Íosa, im chroíse i gcuimhne gach uair,
   bí, a Íosa, in chroíse le haithrí go luath,
   bí, a Íosa, im chroíse le cumann go buan,
   ó, a Íosa, 'Dhé dhílis, ná scar thusa uaim.

2 'Sé Íosa mo ríse, mo chara is mo ghrá;
   'sé Íosa mo dhídean ar pheacaí is ar bhás;
   'sé Íosa mo aoibhneas, mo scáthán de ghnáth;
   is a Íosa, 'Dhé dhílis, ná scar uaim go brách.

3 Bí, a Íosa, go síoraí im chroí is im bhéal,
   bí, a Íosa, go síoraí im thuigse mar an gcéann',
   bí, a Íosa, go síoraí im mheabhair mar léann,
   's ó, a Íosa, 'Dhé dhílis, ná fág mé liom féin.

Anon. (from a manuscript
found in Ulster by Douglas Hyde)

1 *O Jesus, ev'ry moment be in my heart and mind;*
   O Jesus, stir my heart with sorrow for my sins;
   O Jesus, fill my heart with never-failing love;
   O Jesus, sweet Master, never part from me.

2 *O Jesus is my king, my friend, and my love;*
   O Jesus is my shelter from sinning and from death;
   O Jesus, my gladness, my mirror all my days;
   O Jesus, my dearest Lord, never part from me.

3 *O Jesus, be for ever in my heart and my mouth;*
   O Jesus, be for ever in my thought and my prayer;
   O Jesus, be for ever in my quiet mind;
   O Jesus, my sweet Lord, do not leave me alone.

tr. George Otto Simms (b. 1910)

5

ALTERNATIVE ARRANGEMENTS OF HYMNS FROM THE IRISH CHURCH HYMNAL

142 *All my hope on God is founded*

MICHAEL   87 87 337   Herbert Howells (1892–1983)

Irish Church Hymnal No. 492, with alternative tune.

1 All my hope on God is founded;
   he doth still my trust renew,
   me through change and chance he guideth,
   only good and only true,
   God unknown,
   he alone
   calls my heart to be his own.

2 Pride of man and earthly glory,
   sword and crown betray his trust;
   what with care and toil he buildeth,
   tower and temple, fall to dust.
   But God's power,
   hour by hour,
   is my temple and my tower.

3 God's great goodness aye endureth,
   deep his wisdom, passing thought:
   splendour, light, and life attend him,
   beauty springeth out of naught.
   Evermore
   from his store
   new-born worlds rise and adore.

4 Daily doth the almighty giver
   bounteous gifts on us bestow;
   his desire our soul delighteth,
   pleasure leads us where we go.
   Love doth stand
   at his hand;
   joy doth wait on his command.

5 Still from man to God eternal
   sacrifice of praise be done,
   high above all praises praising
   for the gift of Christ his Son.
   Christ doth call
   one and all:
   ye who follow shall not fall.

Joachim Neander (1650–80)
tr. Robert Bridges (1844–1930)

143 *At the name of Jesus*

CAMBERWELL   65 65 D

John Michael Brierley (b. 1932)

An optional variation of *Irish Church Hymnal* No. 373, with alternative tune.
May also be sung to CUDDESDON (No. 132).

Fine   *Optional interlude between verses*   **D.C.**

1 At the name of Jesus every knee shall bow,
   every tongue confess him King of glory now;
   'tis the Father's pleasure we should call him Lord,
   who from the beginning was the mighty Word.

2 At his voice creation sprang at once to sight,
   all the angel faces, all the hosts of light;
   thrones and dominations, stars upon their way,
   all the heavenly orders, in their great array.

3 Humbled for a season, to receive a name
   from the lips of sinners unto whom he came;
   faithfully he bore it spotless to the last,
   brought it back victorious when from death he passed.

4 Bore it up triumphant with its human light,
   through all ranks of creatures to the central height;
   to the eternal Godhead, to the Father's throne,
   filled it with the glory of his triumph won.

5 Name him, Christians, name him, with love strong as death,
   but with awe and wonder, and with bated breath;
   he is God the Saviour, he is Christ the Lord,
   ever to be worshipped, trusted and adored.

6 In your hearts enthrone him; there let him subdue
   all that is not holy, all that is not true;
   crown him as your captain in temptation's hour,
   let his will enfold you in its light and power.

7 With his Father's glory, Jesus comes again,
   angel hosts attend him and announce his reign;
   for all wreaths of empire meet upon his brow,
   and our hearts confess him King of glory now.

Caroline Maria Noel (1817–77)
and in this version Jubilate Hymns

144 *O for a thousand tongues to sing*

LYNGHAM CM extended   Thomas Jarman (1782–1862)

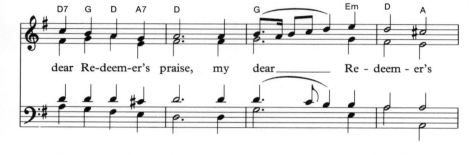

1. O for a thou - sand tongues to___ sing my

dear Re-deem-er's praise, my dear_____ Re - deem - er's

praise, the glo - ries of_____ my God____ and

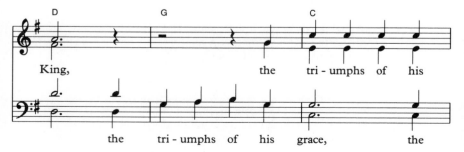

King,   the tri - umphs of his

the tri - umphs of his grace, the

Irish Church Hymnal No. 382, with alternative tune.

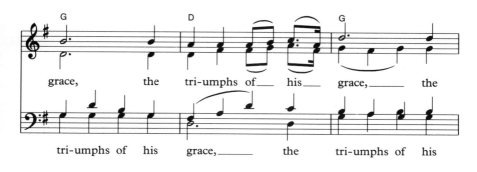

grace, the tri-umphs of__ his__ grace,_____ the

tri-umphs of his grace,_____ the tri-umphs of his

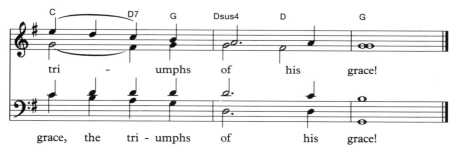

tri - umphs of his grace!

grace, the tri - umphs of his grace!

1 O for a thousand tongues to sing
   my dear Redeemer's praise,
   the glories of my God and King,
   the triumphs of his grace!

2 Jesus! The name that charms our fears,
   that bids our sorrows cease;
   'tis music in the sinner's ears,
   'tis life, and health, and peace.

3 He speaks, and, listening to his voice,
   new life the dead receive,
   the mournful, broken hearts rejoice,
   the humble poor believe.

4 Hear him, ye deaf; his praise, ye dumb,
   your loosened tongues employ:
   ye blind, behold your Saviour come;
   and leap, ye lame, for joy.

5 My gracious Master and my God,
   assist me to proclaim,
   to spread through all the world abroad,
   the honours of thy name.

Charles Wesley (1707–88)

145 *Take my life, and let it be*

NOTTINGHAM   77 77   attrib. Wolfgang Amadeus Mozart (1756–91)

Irish Church Hymnal No. 669, with alternative tune.

1 Take my life, and let it be
  consecrated, Lord, to thee;
  take my moments and my days,
  let them flow in ceaseless praise.

2 Take my hands, and let them move
  at the impulse of thy love;
  take my feet, and let them be
  swift and beautiful for thee.

3 Take my voice, and let me sing
  always, only, for my King;
  take my intellect and use
  every power as thou shalt choose.

4 Take my will, and make it thine;
  it shall be no longer mine;
  take my heart, it is thine own;
  it shall be thy royal throne.

5 Take my love; my Lord, I pour
  at thy feet its treasure store:
  take myself, and I will be
  ever, only, all, for thee.

Frances Ridley Havergal (1836–79)

146 *What a friend we have in Jesus*

CONVERSE 87 87 D

Charles Crozat Converse (1832–1918)

An optional variation of *Irish Church Hymnal* No. 679, with alternative tune.

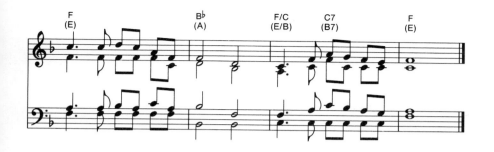

1 What a friend we have in Jesus
   all our sins and griefs to bear,
   what a privilege to carry
   everything to God in prayer;
   O what peace we often forfeit,
   O what needless pain we bear,
   all because we do not carry
   everything to God in prayer!

2 Have we trials and temptations,
   is there trouble anywhere?
   We should never be discouraged:
   take it to the Lord in prayer.
   Can we find a friend so faithful
   who will all our sorrows share?
   Jesus knows our every weakness:
   take it to the Lord in prayer.

3 Are we weak and heavy-laden,
   cumbered with a load of care?
   Jesus is our only refuge:
   take it to the Lord in prayer.
   Do your friends despise, forsake you?
   Take it to the Lord in prayer;
   in his arms he'll take and shield you,
   you will find a solace there.

Joseph Medlicott Scriven (1819–86), altd.

ACKNOWLEDGEMENTS

The Hymnal Revision Committee of the Church of Ireland and Oxford University Press thank the following who have given permission for copyright material to be included. Every effort has been made to trace copyright owners, and the compilers apologize to anyone whose rights have inadvertently not been acknowledged. A blank in the third column indicates that permission has been granted by the author or composer.

WORDS

An asterisk indicates a translation.

Author/Translator	Hymn No.	Text used by permission of
Alternative Prayer Book 1984	127, 131	© 1984, the General Synod of the Church of Ireland, published by Collins
Appleford, P.	113	© Josef Weinberger Ltd.
Barker, O.	41	Thankyou Music
Bayly, A. F.	54, 68	Oxford University Press
Bilbrough, D.	49	Thankyou Music
Blakeley, P.	27	A. & C. Black (Publishers) Ltd., from *Someone's Singing, Lord*
Bowers, J. E.	102	
Brooks, R. T.	80	Hope Publishing Company, USA
Burns, E. J.	93	
Carter, S.	43, 70, 97	Stainer & Bell Ltd.
Chisholm, T. O.	36	Hope Publishing Company, USA
Clark, H.	117	Thankyou Music
Coelho, T.	18	Word (UK) Ltd.
Colvin, T.	46	Hope Publishing Company, USA
Connaughton, L.	109	McCrimmon Publishing Co. Ltd.
Courtney, R.	65	
Cross, S.	16	Exors. of Stewart Cross
Darling, E. F.	126	Oxford University Press/© E. F. Darling
Davison, W. D.	140*	Oxford University Press/© W. D. Davison
Downey, P.	138*	
Dudley-Smith, T.	9, 17, 25, 51, 61, 64, 75, 78, 94, 95, 115, 130, 136, 137	
Dunn, F.	135	Thankyou Music
Ellis, C.	125	Oxford University Press
Evans, D.	7	Thankyou Music
Farjeon, E.	59	David Higham Associates
Fishel, D.	1, 82	The Word of God, USA
Foley, J. B.	24, 122	North American Liturgy Resources, USA
Foley, W. B.	40	Faber Music Ltd.
Gaunt, H. C. A.	73, 123	Oxford University Press
Gillard, R.	99	Thankyou Music
Gillman, B.	10	Thankyou Music
Green, F. Pratt	22, 30, 48, 50, 63, 96, 110	Stainer & Bell Ltd.
Green, M.	86	Cherry Lane Music Ltd.
Hewlett, M.	106	Oxford University Press
Hine, S. K.	66*	Thankyou Music
Houghton, F.	55	Overseas Missionary Fellowship/this version Jubilate Hymns
Hyde, D.	140	D. Sealy
Icarus, P.	85	McCrimmon Publishing Co. Ltd.
Idle, C. M.	38, 132, 133	Jubilate Hymns/© C. M. Idle
ICET	134	Copyright © 1970, 1971, 1975, International Consultation on English Texts
Jabusch, W. F.	29	
Kaan, F. H.	32, 114	Oxford University Press
	119, 121	Stainer & Bell Ltd.
Kendrick, G.	23, 47, 56, 58, 71, 74, 81, 107	Thankyou Music
Kyle, P.	52	Thankyou Music
Lafferty, K.	77	Word (UK) Ltd.
Marshall-Taylor, G.	87	Jubilate Hymns/© G. Marshall-Taylor
McAuley, J. P.	76	Curtis Brown (Australia) Pty. Ltd/© Mrs N. McAuley
Mowbray, D.	14	Stainer & Bell Ltd.
	111	Jubilate Hymns/© D. Mowbray
Nystrom, M.	5	Restoration Music Ltd.
O'Driscoll, T. H.	98	
Old, M.	79	Scripture Union
Owens, J. & C.	28	Music Publishing International Ltd.
Peacey, J. R.	34	Ms M. J. Hancock
Perry, M.	118, 129	Jubilate Hymns/© M. Perry
Porteous, C.	103	Jubilate Hymns/© C. Porteous
Prebble, S.	117	Thankyou Music
Quinn, J.	11, 21, 90, 128	Geoffrey Chapman Ltd.
	19	International Commission on English in the Liturgy Inc.
Ruston, R.	72	McCrimmon Publishing Co. Ltd.
Saward, M.	13	Jubilate Hymns/© M. Saward
Scott, L.	44	Mrs V. Leonard Williams
Seddon, J. E.	33, 84	Jubilate Hymns/© Mrs M. Seddon
Simms, G. O.	138*, 139*, 141*	
Smith, L. Jnr.	42	Thankyou Music

Author/Translator	Hymn No.	Text used by permission of
Stevenson, L. S.	15*	Oxford University Press
Strover, M. C. T.	37	Jubilate Hymns/© C. Strover
Struther, J.	53	Oxford University Press
Temple, S.	57	Franciscan Communications, USA
Timms, G. B.	83	Oxford University Press
Toolan, S.	104	GIA Publications Inc, USA
Verrall, P.	100	Herald Music Services
Westendorf, O.	116	Archdiocese of Philadelphia, USA
	124	World Library Publications Inc., USA
Winslow, J. C.	67	Mrs J. Tyrrell
Wren, B. A.	12, 88, 105	Oxford University Press

MUSIC

An asterisk indicates an arrangement or harmonization.

Composer/Arranger	Hymn No.	Music used by permission of
Allen, H. P.	80	Oxford University Press/© Sir Richard Allen
Appleford, P.	113	© Josef Weinberger Ltd.
Barnard, J.	13, 33	Jubilate Hymns/© J. Barnard
Bilbrough, D.	49	Thankyou Music
Brierley, J. M.	143	© 1960 Josef Weinberger Ltd.
BBC Hymn Book	15*	Oxford University Press
Carter, S.	43, 70, 97	Stainer & Bell Ltd.
Carver, A. F.	4*, 6*, 35*, 91*, 114i, 139*, 141*	Oxford University Press/© A. F. Carver
Coelho, T.	18	Word (UK) Ltd.
Connolly, R.	58, 76	
Courtney, R.	65	
Cutts, P.	61	Oxford University Press
Darling, E. F.	95ii, 137	Oxford University Press/© E. F. Darling
Davison, W. D.	2*, 6*, 11*, 25, 26*, 29*, 31*, 39*, 51, 55*, 59*, 63*, 64*, 67*, 68, 72*, 78*, 79*, 87*, 90*, 95i, 101*, 106*, 108*, 114ii, 126*, 127, 129, 131, 134*, 140*	Oxford University Press/© W. D. Davison
Downey, P.	138*	
Dunn, F.	135	Thankyou Music
Dykes Bower, J.	48	Royal School of Church Music
Evans, D.	7	Thankyou Music
Ferguson, W. H.	132	Oxford University Press
Finlay, K. G.	17	Broomhill Church, Glasgow
Fishel, D.	1, 82	The Word of God, USA
Foley, J. B.	24, 122	New Dawn Music, USA
Gillard, R.	99	Thankyou Music
Gillman, B.	10	Thankyou Music
Gould, A. C. B.	60	Exors. of A. C. Barham Gould
Greatorex, W.	125, 136	Oxford University Press
Green, M.	86	Cherry Lane Music Ltd.
Hammond, M. J.	62	Owner untraced
Harper, D.	27	A. & C. Black (Publishers) Ltd., from Someone's Singing, Lord
Hine, S. K.	66*	Thankyou Music
Howells, H.	142	Novello & Co. Ltd.
Hutchings, A.	19	Canterbury Press Norwich, from the New English Hymnal
Jackson, F.	22	
Kendrick, G.	23, 47, 56, 58, 71, 74, 81, 107	Thankyou Music
Knight, G. H.	124*	Royal School of Church Music
Kreutz, R. E.	116	Archdiocese of Philadelphia, USA
Kyle, P.	52	Thankyou Music
Lafferty, K.	77	Word (UK) Ltd.
Milner, A.	109	McCrimmon Publishing Co. Ltd.
Murray, A. G.	20	
Nicholson, S. H.	128*	Royal School of Church Music
Nystrom, M.	5	Restoration Music Ltd.
Ó Riada, S.	139	P. Ó Riada
Owens, J.	28	Music Publishing International Ltd.
Prebble, S.	41, 117	Thankyou Music
Richardson, N. L.	65*	R. B. Courtney
Routley, E. R.	53*	Oxford University Press
Runyan, W. M.	36	Hope Publishing Co., USA
Sibelius, J.	8	Breitkopf & Härtel, Wiesbaden
Slater, G. A.	105	Oxford University Press
Smith, L. Jnr.	42	Thankyou Music
Strover, M. C. T.	37	Jubilate Hymns/© C. Strover
Taylor, C. V.	16	Oxford University Press
Temple, S.	57	Franciscan Communications, USA
Thalben-Ball, G.	14	Oxford University Press
Toolan, S.	104	GIA Publications Inc., USA
Vaughan Williams, R.	34, 69*, 73*, 98*, 115*, 119*, 120*	Oxford University Press
Verrall, P.	100	Herald Music Services
von Brethorst, L.	45	Word (UK) Ltd.
Warren, N. L.	75, 118	Jubilate Hymns/© N. Warren
Watson, S.	85	
Wilson, J.	88, 110*	Oxford University Press

A GUIDE TO THE CHOICE OF HYMNS
FOR DIFFERENT OCCASIONS

In the following Table, P = hymn based on the Psalm for the day, OT = hymn based on the Old Testament Reading, E = hymn based on the Epistle, and G = hymn based on the Gospel. The number 1 or 2 after the foregoing letters indicates whether the Reading is from Year 1 or Year 2. If there is an option of more than one Reading on any occasion, the choice of Reading is shown by a number in brackets. (HC) indicates that a hymn is suitable for use at the Holy Communion. *ICH = Irish Church Hymnal.*

HYMNS BASED ON THE
LECTIONARY THEMES
(from the Alternative Prayer Book)

9 before Christmas *The Creation*
140 Álainn farraige spéirghlas
    (Beautiful the green-blue sea)
126 All created things
129 Come, worship God
16 Father, Lord of all creation
22 For the fruits of his creation
36 Great is thy faithfulness
56 Lord, the light of your love G1
59 Morning has broken
64 O Christ the same G1
66 O Lord my God!
68 O Lord of every shining constellation
91 This is the day

8 before Christmas *The Fall*
3 And can it be
71 O Lord, the clouds are gathering
76 Seek, O seek the Lord
82 The light of Christ

7 before Christmas *Abraham*
21 Forth in the peace of Christ we go
48 Let every Christian pray
98 Who are we?

6 before Christmas *Moses*
104 I am the Bread of Life G1

5 before Christmas *The Remnant*
7 Be still OT1
123 Praise the Lord (HC)

Advent 1 *The Advent Hope*
29 God has spoken OT2
42 How lovely on the mountains (*Popular version*) OT1
66 O Lord my God
72 Promised Lord
97 When I needed a neighbour G2

Advent 2 *The Word of God*
101 Break thou the bread of life
129 Come, worship God
29 God has spoken
72 Promised Lord
73 Rise and hear!
76 Seek, O seek the Lord OT1
79 Spirit of God
80 Thanks to God

Advent 3 *The Forerunner*
128 Blest be the God P2
42a How lovely on the mountains OT1
72 Promised Lord
74 Rejoice!
85 The voice of God
146 What a friend we have in Jesus E2

Advent 4 *The Annunciation*
50 Long ago, prophets knew G1
72 Promised Lord

55 Lord, you were rich G2
136 Tell out, my soul P2

Christmas Eve
128 Blest be the God G

Christmas Day *The Birth of Christ*
138 Dia do bheath' a naoidhe naoimh
    (All hail and welcome, holy child)
35 Go, tell it on the mountain
69 O sing a song
87 There is singing in the desert

Christmas 1 (YEAR 1) *The Incarnation*
82 The light of Christ

Christmas 1 (YEAR 2) *The Presentation*
130 Faithful vigil ended G

Christmas 2 (YEAR 1) *My Father's House*
105 I come with joy (HC)
53 Lord of all hopefulness

Christmas 2 (YEAR 2) *The Light of the World*
56 Lord, the light of your love
82 The light of Christ

The Epiphany
2 Amazing grace E
129 Come, worship God
56 Lord, the light of your love
55 Lord, you were rich
86 There is a Redeemer E

Epiphany 1 *The Baptism of Jesus*
2 Amazing grace E2
83 The sinless one to Jordan came
96 When Jesus came to Jordan G1

Epiphany 2 *The First Disciples*
73 Rise and hear! OT2
93 We have a gospel
98 Who are we?

Epiphany 3 *Signs of Glory*
134 Holy, holy, holy Lord
104 I am the Bread of Life G2
77 Seek ye first OT2
136 Tell out, my soul
82 The light of Christ E1
92 To God be the glory!

Epiphany 4 *The New Temple*
7 Be still E2
14 Come to us, creative Spirit
30 God is here
84 The Spirit came, as promised

Epiphany 5 *The Wisdom of God*
16 Father, Lord of all creation
68 O Lord of every shining constellation

Epiphany 6 *Parables*
73 Rise and hear!

9 before Easter *Christ the Teacher*
101 Break thou the bread of life
113 Lord Jesus Christ (HC)
60 May the mind of Christ my Saviour
73 Rise and hear! G2

SAINTS' DAYS AND HOLY DAYS

St Matthias *May 14*
24   For you are my God

The Visitation *May 31*
ː36   Tell out, my soul G

St Columba *June 9*
See *ICH* 485 P, 270 OT, 518 E, 468 E, 202, 203

St Barnabas *June 11*
64   O Christ the same P
90   This is my will G

St John Baptist *June 24*
128   Blest be the God G
85   The voice of God

St Peter *June 29*
See *ICH* 505 E, 537 E, 176 G, 554 G,
  196, 198, 423, 449

St Thomas *July 3*
81   The King is among us

St Mary Magdalene *July 22*
59   Morning has broken
81   The King is among us OT

The Transfiguration *August 6*
2   Amazing grace P
7   Be still
56   Lord, the light of your love
82   The light of Christ

St Bartholomew *August 24*
See *ICH* 340 P(2), 288 E, 180

Birth of BVM *September 8*
136   Tell out, my soul P(2) G(1)

St Matthew *September 21*
82   The light of Christ G
93   We have a gospel G

Michaelmas *September 29*
81   The King is among us G

St Luke *October 18*
63   O Christ, the healer
136   Tell out, my soul

St Simon and St Jude *October 28*
See *ICH* 259 OT, 277 E, 449 E, 403 G,
  161 G

All Saints *November 1*
38   Here from all nations E(1)
44   I sing a song of the saints of God
64   O Christ the same P

St Andrew *November 30*
101   Break thou the bread of life
33   Go forth and tell! E

Apostles and Martyrs
133   God, we praise you

SPECIAL OCCASIONS

1. Ember Days (Ministry)
34   Go forth for God
62   O Breath of life G(3)

2. Thanksgiving for Harvest
139   Ag Críost an Síol
    (The seed is Christ's)
126   All created things
22   For the fruits
25   Fruitful trees
36   Great is thy faithfulness
104   I am the Bread of Life G(5)
62   O Breath of life G(5)
77   Seek ye first G(1) G(3)

3. Dedication Festival
14   Come to us, creative Spirit

4. Community and World Peace
51   Lord, for the years
56   Lord, the light of your love
57   Make me a channel
65   O let us spread the pollen of peace
71   O Lord, the clouds are gathering

5. The Unity of the Church
10   Bind us together, Lord
16   Father, Lord of all creation
21   Forth in the peace of Christ we go
84   The Spirit came, as promised
107   Jesus, stand among us
122   One bread, one body
116   You satisfy the hungry heart

6. The Guidance of the Holy Spirit
3   And can it be E(2)
39   He is Lord E(2)
40   Holy Spirit, come, confirm us
48   Let every Christian pray
58   Meekness and majesty E2
122   One bread, one body E(1) (HC)
86   There is a Redeemer
88   There's a spirit in the air
95   When God the Spirit came
96   When Jesus came to Jordan

7. The Spread of the Gospel
21   Forth in the peace of Christ we go
28   God forgave my sin
33   Go forth and tell!
93   We have a gospel

8. The Appointment of a
  Bishop/Incumbent
33   Go forth and tell!
84   The Spirit came, as promised E
90   This is my will

9. A Particular Commemoration
102   Christians, lift your hearts P

10. Mothering Sunday
2   Amazing grace P(3)
102   Christians, lift your hearts E(3)
32   God of Eve and God of Mary
54   Lord of the home
84   The Spirit came, as promised

11. Remembrance Day
51   Lord, for the years
57   Make me a channel
65   O let us spread the pollen of peace
90   This is my will G(2)

HYMNS FOR THE OCCASIONAL
LITURGICAL OFFICES

1. Baptism
17   Father, now behold us
137   Living Lord, our praise we render!
83   The sinless one to Jordan came *(of an adult)*
96   When Jesus came *(of an adult)*

2. Renewal of Baptismal vows
1   Alleluia, alleluia, give thanks
11   Christ be beside me
16   Father, Lord of all creation
137   Living Lord, our praise we render!
82   The light of Christ
94   We turn to Christ anew

3. Confirmation
(see also hymns for Pentecost)
142   All my hope
9   Be strong in the Lord E(2)
141   Bí, a Íosa, im chroíse
    (O Jesus, every moment)

INDEX OF AUTHORS, TRANSLATORS, AND SOURCES OF TEXTS

INDEX OF COMPOSERS, ARRANGERS, AND SOURCES OF MUSIC

An asterisk indicates a harmonization or arrangement.

INDEX OF TUNES AND METRES

R indicates a refrain. No indication is shown against tunes of irregular metre.

314

INDEX OF FIRST LINES AND TITLES

Where titles differ from first lines they are shown in italic. An asterisk indicates English singing translations of the Irish hymns.